Religious Liberty: Continuity or Contradiction?

The question of religious liberty is no longer a matter of interest only to political philosophers. By the ambiguity of its teaching, the Second Vatican Council elevated the issue to one that concerns all Catholics inasmuch as it touches on the consistency and reliability of the Church herself in her official teaching. Fr. Lucien's work makes an important contribution to resolving the question in favor of that consistency and reliability.

—Dr. John Joy, author of *On the Ordinary &*
Extraordinary Magisterium: From Joseph Kleutgen
to the Second Vatican Council

Many Catholics have been disturbed by an apparent contradiction between the teaching of the Vatican II declaration on religious liberty *Dignitatis Humanæ* and more than one document of the prior magisterium. As a result several writers have offered competing solutions to this apparent contradiction. This present work consists of three essays with two by Fr. Bernard Lucien setting forth his own carefully argued approach. And until one particular solution gains more widespread acceptance as the most probable answer to this difficulty, it is good that theologians and philosophers continue to study and debate this important question that goes to the heart of the Church's ability to know and define truth.

—Thomas Storck, author of *Foundations of*
a Catholic Political Order

Fr. Bernard Lucien is considered one of the best French traditionalist theologians. His explanation of religious liberty has three merits in my eyes: it is simple and clear; it is based on the literal meaning of the text of *Dignitatis*

Humanæ, and it displays a truly traditional spirit. Let us hope that, thanks to this publication, it will receive greater recognition.

—**Fr. Louis-Marie de Blignières**, founder, Fraternity of
St. Vincent Ferrer (Chémeré-le-Roi, France)

This book makes an original and valuable contribution to the debate on religious liberty. It deserves to be read by all who wish to understand *Dignitatis Humanæ* and the duty of human societies "toward the true religion and toward the one Church of Christ."

—**Fr. Thomas Crean**, O.P., co-author with
Dr. Alan Fimister of *Integralism: A Manual
of Political Philosophy*

Father Lucien began studying the conciliar declaration *Dignitatis Humanæ* in order to demonstrate its incompatibility with traditional teaching. This search for truth, however, led him to reverse his previous position and to find a way out in full agreement with classical moral theology. Analyzing the differing concepts of "conscience" occurring in Western thought since Aquinas, he concluded that the "liberty of conscience and cult" condemned by the nineteenth-century popes was something much more radical and sweeping than the right to religious freedom affirmed by Vatican II. While some of us who have reached the same conclusion have arrived at it by a rather different path from Fr. Lucien, giving more attention to the "due limits" to religious freedom affirmed by *DH*, his work is a serious contribution to this *quaestio disputata* that deserves the attention of every theologian.

—**Fr. Brian W. Harrison**, OS, STD, author of
Religious Liberty and Contraception

Religious Liberty: Continuity or Contradiction?

READING *DIGNITATIS HUMANÆ* WITHIN TRADITION

By Fr. Bernard Lucien

with commentary by
Fr. Antoine-Marie de Araujo, FSVF

Translated by
John Pepino, Ph.D.

Foreword by
Alan Fimister, Ph.D.

AROUCA
PRESS

CONTENTS

TRANSLATOR'S NOTE

The three articles we here present constitute a reflection on a controversial teaching of Vatican II: religious liberty as defined in *Dignitatis Humanæ*, no. 2. This teaching has caused difficulty to many Catholics, to the point that some are in imperfect communion with the Holy See, if not sedevacantists. The reader will determine whether he finds the arguments in the following two articles by Fr. Bernard Lucien and that by Fr. Antoine-Marie de Araujo, FSVF, convincing; certainly they will contribute to the conversation on a controverted topic. The issue is whether *Dignitatis Humanæ* contradicts prior magisterial teaching. Fr. Lucien and Fr. Araujo argue that it does not.

It may be well to provide the context in which the principal author, Fr. Bernard Lucien, came to the reflections in the pages to follow.

Born in 1952,[1] a young Bernard Lucien received a Catholic education from the Marist brothers before attending preparatory school and the School of Mines in Saint-Étienne. He entered Archbishop Lefebvre's seminary at Écône in 1972. He was ordained a subdeacon there in June 1977 but had to leave the seminary shortly thereafter because of his agreement with Fr. Guérard des Lauriers's thesis that the Holy See was formally vacant. He

---

[1] The following bibliographical indications are drawn from Yves Chiron, "Dictionnaire biographique des Catholiques de Tradition," in idem, *Histoire des Traditionalistes suivie d'un dictionnaire biographique* (Paris: Tallandier, 2022), s.v. "Lucien, Bernard," 518–19.

(along with his confrere Hervé Belmont, who shared his views) was sent to live with Fr. Aulagnier, then French district superior of the SSPX. Archbishop Lefebvre ordained Bernard Lucien deacon in April 1978 in Vichy and priest in June of the same year at Écône along with his classmates.

As a young priest, Fr. Lucien was instrumental in broadcasting Fr. Guérard des Lauriers's thesis through a publication he launched with Fr. Seuillot in 1979: *Les Cahiers de Cassiciacum* (it had a total run of six issues, until April 1981); in fact, the "formal vacancy" thesis came to be called the "Cassiciacum thesis." From 1981 to 1995, he lived in independent priories.

In 1984, Fr. Lucien published a work seeking to demonstrate "the existence of a daily infallible exercise of the Church's Magisterium."[2] He then turned his attention to religious liberty: in 1988 (co-author: Fr. Hervé Belmont) with *La Liberté religieuse*,[3] and in 1990 with *Grégoire XVI, Pie IX et Vatican II*.[4] In both works, Fr. Lucien sought to demonstrate the contradiction between the teaching of Gregory XVI and Pius IX on "freedom of conscience and worship" and the teaching of Vatican II on religious liberty.

He fundamentally changed his view (a change for which he credits the grace of God) on Christmas 1991 and published a retraction in 1992 to show how this contradiction was merely apparent and not substantial. This led him to regularize his canonical status in 1992; he was incardinated in the archdiocese of Vaduz (Liechtenstein) in 2004

[2] Bernard Lucien, *L'infaillibilité du magistère ordinaire et universel de l'Église* (Nice, France: Association Saint-Herménégilde, 1984).

[3] Hervé Belmont and Bernard Lucien, *La Liberté religieuse. Examen d'une tentative de justification. Réponse au Prieuré Saint-Thomas d'Aquin* (Paris: Association Saint-Jérôme, 1988).

[4] Bernard Lucien, *Grégoire XVI, Pie IX et Vatican II. Études sur la liberté religieuse dans la doctrine catholique* (Tours, France: Forts dans la foi, 1990).

by Archbishop Haas. Since his regularization he has been teaching in houses of formation in full communion with the Holy See and publishing works of theology,[5] including for the non-specialist public.[6]

Since the 1992 retraction was not well known, Fr. Lucien, inspired by Benedict XVI's 2005 Address to the Roman Curia on the "hermeneutic of continuity,"[7] agreed to publish his reflections in *Sedes Sapientiæ*, the review of the Fraternity of Saint Vincent Ferrer (based in Chémeré-le-Roi, France).[8] That is the first article of the three we here republish.

The second article republished below is a response to an objector, Fr. Christophe Héry, IBP, who provided Fr. Lucien with the opportunity to partly clarify this thought.[9]

The third article, originally published in 2019, is by Fr. Lucien's disciple, Fr. Antoine-Marie de Araujo, FSVF, who further explains the compatibility between *Dignitatis Humanæ* and the Church's preconciliar magisterial teaching.[10]

On a personal note, I should add that like many Catholics attached to the traditional teaching, liturgy, and devotional life of the Church, I have friends and acquaintants (clerical

---

[5] Idem, *Les Degrés d'autorité du Magistère* (Vaulx-en-Velin, France: La Nef, 2007).

[6] Idem, *Théologie sacrée pour débutants et initiés*, 3 vols. (Greux, France: 2007–2011).

[7] Benedict XVI, Address to the Roman Curia (December 22, 2005), *Acta Apostolicæ Sedis* 98 (2006): 40–53.

[8] Bernard Lucien, "Vatican II et 'l'herméneutique de la continuité': le cas crucial de la liberté religieuse," *Sedes Sapientiæ* 96 (2006): 3–22.

[9] Idem, "Petite suite sur la liberté religieuse et Vatican II," *Sedes Sapientiæ* 97 (2007): 19–39, a response to Christophe Héry, "Vraie tolérance et fausse liberté religieuse. Le problème crucial de l'abbé B. Lucien," *Mascaret* 281 (July–August 2006): 6–7.

[10] Antoine-Marie de Araujo, "En définissant la liberté religieuse, Vatican II a-t-il contredit le magistère antérieur? Une solution proposée par l'abbé Lucien," *Sedes Sapientiæ* 147 (March 2019).

and lay) who live their faith in imperfect communion with the Holy See, and others who live radically outside of that communion. Their position rests on the apparent contradiction between *Dignitatis Humanæ* no. 2 and the Church's perennial teaching on freedom of conscience. It is my hope that Fr. Lucien's and Fr. Araujo's deep and nuanced thought on the matter will help resolve that misapprehension by showing that *Dignitatis Humanæ* leaves the door open to some kind of legitimate constraint in defense of the true religion as such.

JOHN PEPINO
Lincoln, Nebraska
Feast of St. John Eudes, 2024

FOREWORD

Alan Fimister, Ph.D.

"Two shall be in the field. One shall be taken and one shall be left. Two women shall be grinding at the mill. One shall be taken and one shall be left. Watch ye therefore, because you know not what hour your Lord will come" (Matt 20:40–22)

In Article 3 of Question 5 of the *Secunda Secundæ* St. Thomas asks "Whether a man who disbelieves one article of faith, can have lifeless faith in the other articles?" His answer is a categorical "no."

> Neither living nor lifeless faith remains in a heretic who disbelieves one article of faith. The reason of this is that the species of every habit depends on the formal aspect of the object, without which the species of the habit cannot remain. Now the formal object of faith is the First Truth, as manifested in Holy Writ and the teaching of the Church, which proceeds from the First Truth. Consequently whoever does not adhere, as to an infallible and Divine rule, to the teaching of the Church, which proceeds from the First Truth manifested in Holy Writ, has not the habit of faith, but holds that which is of faith otherwise than by faith.[1]

---

[1] *Summa Theologiæ*, IIa IIæ, 5, 3.

Over the last sixty years the faithful have had the opportunity to observe this phenomenon on a massive scale in sermons, newspapers, religious literature, architecture and in everyday conversation.

When Pope Paul VI said of the last ecumenical council that "it avoided issuing solemn dogmatic definitions engaging the infallibility of the ecclesiastical Magisterium,"[2] he did not mean that Vatican II issued no infallible teaching, simply that it issued no new infallible teaching specifically identified as divinely revealed. In practice, as Joseph Ratzinger observed in 1988, the Second Vatican Council has been treated "as though it made itself into a sort of super-dogma which takes away the importance of all the rest."[3]

The effect of this has been to create two vast reservoirs of apostates: those who think the Council definitively contradicted equally definitive teaching issued by prior councils and popes and lament the fact, and those who think the Council definitively contradicted equally definitive teaching issued by prior councils and popes and rejoice. Neither group (for the reasons St. Thomas explains) possess the theological virtue of faith[4] and therefore neither group possesses the theological virtues of hope or charity either. The consequences of that are set out in detail by St. Thérèse of Lisieux.

[2] Paul VI, General Audience, January 12, 1966.
[3] Joseph Cardinal Ratzinger, "Address to the Bishops of Chile," July 13, 1988.
[4] As the First Vatican Council teaches "the situation of those, who by the heavenly gift of faith have embraced the Catholic truth, is by no means the same as that of those who, led by human opinions, follow a false religion; for those who have accepted the faith under the guidance of the Church can never have any just cause for changing this faith or for calling it into question." *Dei Filius* (1870).

I saw that if the Church was a body made up of different members, the most essential and important one of all would not be lacking; I saw that the Church must have a heart, that this heart must be on fire with love. I saw that it was love alone which moved her other members, and that were this love to fail, apostles would no longer spread the Gospel, and martyrs would refuse to shed their blood.[5]

The Heart of the Church, the Heart of the God-man, beats still, but countless extremities of the visible body are no longer reached by the charity which is its life blood.

For many ordinary people the occasion of this calamity was the transformation and abuse of the liturgy or even of disciplinary practice. A group of priests I addressed a few years ago reported that they had met and thankfully reconciled many elderly lapsed Catholics who abandoned the Church when Friday abstinence was discontinued. For many more theologically informed individuals, however, the stone of stumbling was religious liberty.

The *Catechism of the Catholic Church* section 890 assures us that,

> The mission of the Magisterium is linked to the definitive nature of the covenant established by God with his people in Christ. It is this Magisterium's task to preserve God's people from deviations and defections and to guarantee them the objective possibility of professing the true faith without error.[6]

---

[5] St. Thérèse of Lisieux, *The Story of a Soul*, trans. Michael Day (Charlotte, NC: St. Benedict Press, 2010), 163.

[6] CCC (1997) §890.

If the faithful and their pastors for over a thousand years held (and they surely did) that the Church had the right to employ coercion and even lethal force to correct erring members of the faithful, and they were in fact wrong, then this claim is completely empty and with it Christ's teaching that the Church is a city set upon a hill that cannot be hidden, and His promise to remain with her until the end of time.[7]

If the teaching of the ordinary and universal or the extraordinary Magisterium can and has contradicted itself, then this does not mean that the new teaching is true or that the Church has foundered, but that Catholicism was never true and we are of all men most to be pitied.[8]

The task of reconciling the declaration *Dignitatis Humanæ* and the previous definitions and tradition of the Church is therefore no trifling matter. Upon it hinges the credibility of Catholicism itself.

There are those of course who hold that *Dignitatis Humanæ* does indeed err but that it is not definitive.[9] They are mistaken. Even were we to entertain their claim as a hypothesis, the consequences would remain if not fatal at least devastating, as it would mean that the authentic Magisterium in its highest expression had erred for more than half a century in such a way as virtually to eclipse its reliability altogether. Obviously, the situation in which the Church militant finds itself of late is not irreconcilable with such a hypothesis but it is unclear how it would be reconciled with the aforementioned words of Our Lord at the end of the first gospel.[10]

---

[7] Matthew 5:14; 28:20.

[8] 1 Corinthians 15:19.

[9] For example: Michael Davies, *The Second Vatican Council and Religious Liberty* (Long Prairie, MN: Neumann Press, 1992).

[10] "When it comes to the question of interventions in the prudential order, it could happen that some Magisterial documents might not

Those who insist (rightly) that *Dignitatis Humanæ* does not contradict the ordinary and universal Magisterium or the definitions of *Quanta Cura* are faced with a stark difficulty which may be illustrated by placing side by side the definitions of the latter with that of *Dignitatis Humanæ*.

> against the doctrine of Scripture, of the Church, and of the Holy Fathers, they do not hesitate to assert that 'that is the best condition of civil society, in which no duty is recognized, as attached to the civil power, of restraining by enacted penalties, offenders against the Catholic religion, except so far as public peace may require.[11]

> by our Apostolic authority, we reprobate, proscribe, and condemn all the singular and evil opinions and doctrines severally mentioned in this letter, and will and command that they be thoroughly held by all children of the Catholic Church as reprobated, proscribed and condemned.[12]

> This Vatican Council declares that the human person has a right to religious freedom. This freedom means that all men are to be immune from coercion on the part of individuals or of social groups and of any human power, in such wise that no one is to be forced to act in

be free from all deficiencies. Bishops and their advisors have not always taken into immediate consideration every aspect or the entire complexity of a question. But it would be contrary to the truth, if, proceeding from some particular cases, one were to conclude that the Church's Magisterium can be habitually mistaken in its prudential judgments, or that it does not enjoy divine assistance in the integral exercise of its mission." Congregation for the Doctrine of the Faith, *Donum Veritatis Instruction on the Ecclesial Vocation of the Theologian* (1990) §24.

[11] Pius IX, *Quanta Cura* (1864) D1689.

[12] Pius IX, *Quanta Cura* (1864) D1699.

a manner contrary to his own beliefs, whether privately
or publicly, whether alone or in association with others,
within due limits.[13]

The difficulty in reconciling these statements is obvious,
although St. John Henry Newman set a sterling example
in his own day of submission and precise construction of
both *Quanta Cura* and the (less authoritative) *Syllabus*
for later men to follow. Those who have attempted to
reconcile *Dignitatis Humanæ* and *Quanta Cura* have generally followed one of three (not incompatible) paths.
Some have focused upon the concluding phrase "within
due limits." Led by Thomas Pink, others more recently
have focused upon the expression "human power."[14] The
present work focuses instead upon the implications of the
words "contrary to his own beliefs." Catholic theologians
ought to be practiced in distinguishing between the minis-
ter, object and the circumstances of some act of order or
jurisdiction and the central phrase invites us to make the
same distinctions here.

Each of these approaches is legitimate and fruitful and
does justice to the proper rules of magisterial construction
but the third of them has a special importance which is
very often missed. It is missed because even Catholics can
sleepwalk into treating the faith in a liberal manner as if it
were one opinion among many and capable of reasonable
doubt. For those who have not yet received the grace of
justifying faith, who can judge the hidden fault of incredu-
lity? Despite the overwhelming marks of credibility which
attend the gospel, it remains the case that "eye hath not
seen, nor ear heard, neither hath it entered into the heart

[13] Second Vatican Ecumenical Council, *Dignitatis Humanæ* (1965) §2.
[14] Thomas Pink, "The Interpretation of Dignitatis Humanæ: A Reply
to Martin Rhonheimer," 2013, *Nova et Vetera*, English Edition, Vol.
11, No. 1 (2013).

of man, what things God hath prepared for them that love him"[15] and God "hath mercy on whom he will; and whom he will, he hardeneth."[16] We cannot forget that "by grace you are saved through faith: and that not of yourselves, for it is the gift of God."[17] Woe to him who would seek to wrest that gift from God's hand by temporal power. In baptism, however, God has handed over to men the "power to be made the sons of God."[18]

As the Catechism reminds us (using the words of both St. John Henry Newman and St. Thomas),

> Faith is certain. It is more certain than all human knowledge because it is founded on the very word of God who cannot lie. To be sure, revealed truths can seem obscure to human reason and experience, but "the certainty that the divine light gives is greater than that which the light of natural reason gives." "Ten thousand difficulties do not make one doubt."[19]

It is for this reason that the Apostle, without needing to read any man's soul, can say with certainty that the heretic is acting *against* his own conscience and his own beliefs, "A man that is a heretic, after the first and second admonition, avoid: Knowing that he that is such an one is subverted and sinneth, being condemned by his own judgment."[20]

Does that mean *Dignitatis Humanæ* is essentially disingenuous? That it sounds and intends to sound as if it is excluding coercion from religious questions when it is

---

[15] 1 Corinthians 2:9.
[16] Romans 9:18.
[17] Ephesians 2:8.
[18] John 1:12.
[19] CCC (1997) §157.
[20] Titus 3:10–11.

doing no such thing? I do not think the Catholic student of this question is compelled to exclude in principle the possibility that the document might be viewed in this way. On the other hand, it is here that analysis of the Declaration as (in its novel aspects) an implicit statement of ecclesiastical policy rather than doctrine plays a crucial role. Also key is the second claim which is made the object of a "declaration" by the Council: "The council further declares that the right to religious freedom has its foundation in the very dignity of the human person as this dignity is known through the revealed word of God and by reason itself." The exact nature of that dignity and therefore the extent to which it is knowable and founded upon reason and nature, and the extent to which it is knowable and founded upon revelation and grace naturally affect the relative competences of the temporal and spiritual powers. This was of course a question which raged before during and after the Council itself and is not settled in any way by this or any other of the documents of Vatican II.

Magisterial documents, though strengthened against error and, when definitive, preserved from it, are not inspired in the same sense as scripture: "we have this treasure in earthen vessels."[21] The Lord promised Peter that his faith would not fail,[22] not that his words would always be opportune or (in the case of his successors) even true. The painstaking distinctions and careful exegesis of Fr. Lucien are the proper and Catholic response when either subjectively or objectively a teaching presents itself as both authoritative (in whatever degree) and perplexing. As Newman admonished us a century and half ago when distinguishing between the authority of the *Syllabus* and the Encyclical of 1864 and meticulously parsing the teaching

[21] 2 Corinthians 4:7.
[22] Luke 22:32.

of the latter, "When intelligence which we receive from Rome startles and pains us from its seemingly harsh or extreme character, let us learn to have some little faith and patience, and not take for granted that all that is reported is the truth."[23]

---

[23] St. John Henry Newman, *A Letter Addressed to the Duke of Norfolk on Occasion of Mr. Gladstone's Recent Expostulation* (London: Longmans, Green, And Co., 1900) 280.

ONE

Vatican II and the "Hermeneutic of Continuity": The Crucial Case of Religious Liberty[†]

Fr. Bernard Lucien

Much ink has been spilled in all sectors of the Church on the question of religious liberty at the Second Vatican Council and its relationship to earlier magisterial teaching. One fact is worth noting for the leaders of the so-called "traditionalist" movement: four theologians of their school of thought undertook the study of this issue by taking as their starting point the view that Vatican II was in formal contradiction *with the earlier Magisterium of the Church. After in-depth studies, and through different— sometimes even opposed—paths, they ultimately concluded that, despite the significant deficiencies of the declaration* Dignitatis Humanæ, *which sets out the Church's doctrine on this point in the last Council, there existed no such contradiction. These theologians are Father Brian*

[†] An earlier version of this text was published in *Sedes Sapientiæ* 96 (2006), 3–22.

Harrison,[1] some of the editors at Sedes Sapientiæ,[2] *Father Basile Valuet,[3] and Father Bernard Lucien.*

Sedes Sapientiæ *published the following, which concords with some of Father Victor-Alain Berto's views: "One may then say that the declaration is weak, equivocal, dangerous, yet not erroneous in its main teaching.[4] It is weak in its considerations: some are highly conditioned by their historical and cultural context as well as by a fairly unrealistic view of things that forgets the concrete conditions of the exercise of freedom as weakened by sin and also forgets the perversity of some of the forces before which the weak are defenseless. It is equivocal in several of its expressions; so much so that, despite the Relator's explanations at the Council, it is invoked to justify the emancipation of theologians from the Magisterium. It is especially dangerous because its omissions expose it to indifferentist interpretations. In its central assertion, however . . .* Dignitatis Humanæ *does not contradict the*

---

[1] Brian W. Harrison, OSS, *Religious Liberty and Contraception* (Melbourne: John XXIII Fellowship, 1988). See also idem, "Pius IX, Vatican II and Religious Liberty," *Living Tradition* 9 (January 1987), accessible online at www.rtforum.org/lt/lt9.html#11 [accessed 7/13/2024].

[2] Louis-Marie de Blignières and Dominique-Marie de Saint Laumer, "Nos recherches sur la liberté religieuse" and "Le droit à la liberté religieuse et la liberté de conscience," *Sedes Sapientiæ* 22 (Winter 1988), Supplement.

[3] Basile Valuet, OSB, *La liberté religieuse et la Tradition catholique* (Le Barroux: Abbaye Sainte-Madeleine, 2nd ed., 1998), 6 volumes.

[4] The *Relator* [in response to a modus proposed by 44 Fathers—*trans.*] declared that the teaching alone was proposed *auctoritative*: Modus ad numerum 2: . . . . *[U]t non videatur argumentatio auctoritative a S. Synodo proponi.* . . . R. *[U]t clarius appareat quod argumentatio non auctoritate proponitur,* "It must be clear that the argumentation is not proposed with authority," *Acta Synodalia Sacrosancti Concilii Œcumenici Vaticani Secundi* (Vatican City: Typis Polygottis Vaticanis, 1978), IV, VI, 735.

prior Magisterium and even presents a homogeneous development of the doctrine on social order."[5]

At the time Sedes Sapientiæ *called for a "theological fight" for the correct interpretation of the central teaching of* Dignitatis Humanæ *as well as for a correction of its deficiencies. The ongoing debates within the Church about Tradition and the secularist depredations in society confirm the timeliness of the call issued eighteen years ago.*
—*The editors of* Sedes Sapientiæ, *June 2006.*

The now-famous address His Holiness Pope Benedict XVI gave to the Roman Curia on December 22, 2005[6] called upon all the faithful to receive the Second Vatican Council not according to a hermeneutic of rupture and discontinuity with earlier magisterial teaching, but in a spirit of continuity and harmony that remains open to legitimate developments and reforms. One who has closely studied the texts of this most recent ecumenical council will be aware that while many passages may allow for interpretations of rupture, one alone truly *seems*, in its most literal reading, *irreducible* to previous doctrine: the definition of the right to religious liberty as formulated in the middle of the second section of the declaration *Dignitatis Humanæ*.

As for me, I thought I had established with great precision the *reality* of this *apparent contradiction* in a study

5   L.-M. de Blignières, "Nos recherches sur la liberté religieuse," *Sedes Sapientiæ* 22 (Winter 1988), Supplement.

6   Benedict XVI, Address to the Roman Curia (December 22, 2005), *Acta Apostolicæ Sedis* 98 (2006), 40–53, accessible at https://www. vatican.va/content/benedict-xvi/en/speeches/2005/december/documents/hf_ben_xvi_spe_20051222_roman-curia.html [accessed 07/29/2024]

published in 1990,[7] the result of work undertaken about ten years earlier. Yet, by the grace of God, towards the end of December 1991 I came across an essential element that had not been brought out by those who have written on the subject. It invalidated my work's conclusion.

In March 1992 I published a retraction regarding the *conclusion* of my study on religious liberty. But the circumstances at the time did not allow for a broad dissemination of this clarification beyond readers known to me personally. The climate that the Holy Father's address has created in the Church incites me to respond to the request of *Sedes Sapientiæ*. I shall thus be in a position to spread farther abroad, through this journal, a presentation that may contribute to current efforts aiming at the return to full doctrinal clarity of those subjects that have been obscured in the past few decades.[8]

1. The apparent contradiction and its unsatisfactory solutions

The apparent contradiction between the Vatican II declaration and the earlier doctrine consists in this: according to Vatican II, man has a natural right to act freely (i.e., free

---

[7] Bernard Lucien, *Grégoire XVI, Pie IX et Vatican II. Études sur la liberté religieuse dans la doctrine catholique* (Tours: Forts dans la Foi, 1990). As the title of this work indicates, it sought to examine the issue of compatibility between the teaching of the Vatican II declaration *Dignitatis Humanæ* on religious liberty and earlier Catholic doctrine as solemnly affirmed by Gregory XVI and Pius IX. Henceforth I shall refer to it as *BL* followed by the page number.

[8] For readers familiar with my study, I should specify that my radical change of view regarding the ultimate conclusion does not necessarily render entirely useless the many analyses in the body of the work. The present clarification will provide the reader with the necessary indications for discerning and rectifying error, all the while retaining that which—I hope—remains valid.

from human constraint) in the religious sphere, whereas Gregory XVI and Pius IX denied the existence of such a natural right.[9]

My book examined the various serious attempts[10] at resolving this contradiction that had been published at the time of writing. I showed the insufficiency of Fr Harrison's thesis and of the works that Frs. de Blignières and de Saint Laumer built on it.

Regarding the issue under discussion, their thesis was supposed to resolve the contradiction essentially on the basis of the "necessary limits" mentioned in the text of *Dignitatis Humanæ*. I showed that, according to its actual meaning in the very text of Vatican II, this restrictive mention does not, in my opinion, remove the opposition with earlier teaching.

I think that this aspect of my work retains all its relevance. Indeed, the trail blazed by Fr. Harrison was accepted by several authors who have written since, sometimes with a remarkable erudition worthy of admiration.[11] In my view, however, once one goes down that path in an attempt to resolve the apparent contradiction, he finds himself obliged to minimize Catholic doctrine as defined in the nineteenth century in full continuity with earlier, age-old

---

[9] For Vatican II, see the central affirmation in the Declaration on Religious Freedom *Dignitatis Humanæ* no. 2 (*BL* 244); for Gregory XVI, the essential text is paragraph 14 of his Encyclical *Mirari Vos* (*BL* 10–11); for Pius IX, see the statement in the third paragraph of his Encyclical *Quanta Cura* (*BL* 123–25).

[10] That is, those attempts that examined the actual issue without distracting attention towards subjects that are not directly at issue, such as the freedom of the act of faith, indifferentism, the Christian State, what prudential judgment ought to apply to the present world situation, etc.

[11] Readers familiar with the literature on the topic will have seen that what I say here also applies, generally speaking, to Fr. Basile Valuet's position in his monumental thesis, *La liberté religieuse*.

practice and teaching. Moreover, those authors who least minimize this earlier doctrine do not really respect the meaning of the "necessary limits" as found in the text of *Dignitatis Humanæ*.

Therefore, on this point—which is at the heart of my book—I stand by my arguments and the conclusions deduced from them.

This is only to mention those positions that contrast with mine; indeed, the purpose of this article is simply to propose an interpretation that seems truly to fit the hermeneutic of continuity while underscoring the legitimate development of Vatican II.

2. The principle of resolution

In my view, the essential difference between the right affirmed by *Dignitatis Humanæ* and that condemned by Gregory XVI and Pius IX consists in this:

- *Dignitatis Humanæ* affirms the natural right to the [external] liberty to act, in religious matters, *according to one's conscience*;

- the two popes mentioned above deny the existence of a natural right to the external liberty to act, in religious matters, *as one wishes*.[12]

Indeed, it is quite possible, and alas very common, for a man to act *as he wishes*, though not *according to his conscience*. In fact, one who sins often acts *against his conscience*, whereas in other cases he acts *according to his*

---

[12] It is easy to verify these two affirmations by referring to the central sentence of *Dignitas Humanæ* for the first and to the first two chapters of my book for the second. See also the "complementary technical precisions" below.

culpably erroneous conscience. It can even happen that man, hardened to the point of indifference towards good and evil, acts *absent any judgment of conscience.*

Moreover, the judgment of conscience in every man is exercised by practical reason, which first apprehends the general principles of the moral order. This knowledge of universal principles is *per se* accessible to every human intelligence. This objective accessibility also applies to the *fact* of divine Revelation fulfilled and completed in Jesus Christ, since this Revelation is accompanied by signs of credibility that are both highly certain and also adapted to the intelligence of all men.[13] To be sure, knowledge of the general principles of morality and religion vary from one person to the next, according to the circumstances of social background, upbringing, and other more individual factors. But these diverse circumstances, which shape one's access to the knowledge of general and universal principles, are *of themselves observable from the outside.*

Therefore, at least *in part* and *in certain cases*, it is possible to form a prudential judgment from the outside (supposing one has a legitimate reason to do so) regarding whether someone is acting according to his conscience or not.[14]

---

[13] This last assertion, so often unknown to modern authors, is explicitly formulated by Vatican I, Dogmatic Constitution on the Catholic Faith *Dei Filius* (April 24, 1870), 3.2: "Nevertheless, in order that the obedience of our faith might be in accordance with reason (Rom. 12:1), it was God's will that there should be linked to the internal assistance of the Holy Spirit outward indications of His revelation, that is to say divine acts, and first and foremost miracles and prophecies, which clearly demonstrating as they do the omnipotence and infinite knowledge of God, are the most certain signs of Revelation, and are suited to the understanding of all." Norman P. Tanner, SJ, ed., *Decrees of the Ecumenical Councils*, vol. 2, *Trent to Vatican II* (London: Sheed and Ward, and Washington DC: Georgetown University Press, 1990), 807.

[14] While this assertion offends contemporary subjectivism, it certainly belongs to the realism of Christian thought, particularly to the philosophical and theological doctrine of St. Thomas as well as to the

Those who wish to study this aspect further will refer to the classic discussions on the notion of just war.[15] It clearly emerges that, even though many theologians from the sixteenth century on sought to mitigate this doctrine, the authors of the Middle Ages, most prominently St. Thomas, demanded the proven culpability of the adversary as one of the conditions for just war. This demonstrates that for these soundly realist theologians, it is not necessarily impossible to make a legitimate judgment about the state of another person's conscience—not a judgment endowed with the infallibility of divine knowledge, to be sure, but one that can reach the level of the moral certitude required for human acts in a grave matter.

Hence the right to act *as one wishes* not only is formally different from the right to act *according to one's conscience*, but in fact grants far more—at least under some societal circumstances—in terms of exemption from constraint.[16]

There is, then, no contradiction between the condemnation of the former and the assertion of the latter.

3. Overview of the Church's praxis

The central assertion of *Dignitatis Humanæ*,[17] understood as I have presented it here, does not substantially call into question the Church's praxis throughout Christendom.

teaching and practice of the Church. Note that it is not enough to accept the distinction I made at the outset; one must also acknowledge the truth of this assertion to remove the apparent contradiction between *Dignitatis Humanæ* and the earlier doctrine.

[15] The entry point to the study of this theme will be found in the summaries Fr. J.-A. Robilliard, OP, published in the *Bulletin Thomiste* 4.6 (April–June 1935): 433–36 and 5.7 (July-September 1938): 449–53.

[16] In this I had anticipated the objection of Fr. Basile, vol.1.B, 705n3025. See also the further considerations here at no. 3.

[17] I here refer to the sentence that defines the right to religious liberty in *Dignitatis Humanæ Personæ* no. 2. Indeed, I hold that, as Fr. Guérard des Lauriers, OP, established in *Les Cahiers de Cassiciacum* 1, this

Indeed conscience, according to Catholic theology,[18] has as its proper function the *application* of the general norms of morality to a *particular* act that the subject is considering performing.[19] Therefore, even though an acting person may *not have taken into account the objective general moral data* (be they natural or supernatural) that are *actually available to him*, the fact remains that *legitimate authority* may *legitimately presume* that the person in question *is not acting according to his conscience*.

Now the Catholic religion has grounds of credibility that are "suited to the understanding of all";[20] in *the context of Christendom*, these data are indeed within everybody's reach. The Church, therefore, has been in a position legitimately to presume that those who did not take them into account (heretics and the like, or, in a different way, infidels intending to spread their errors in a Catholic nation) were not acting according to their conscience.[21]

---

assertion of itself is guaranteed by infallibility. On the other hand, I hold that other passages in that declaration may (from the point of view of Catholic doctrine on the Magisterium and the adhesion it requires), and indeed deserve (by their literal content), to be critiqued (see the end of this article).

[18] *Veritatis Splendor* (August 6, 1993), no. 59 recalls this realist Catholic doctrine. Since this notion of the judgment of conscience is the keystone of my interpretation of the right to religious liberty in *Dignitatis Humanæ*, one may see in this later papal determination a valuable confirmation of the non-arbitrariness of my reading. Here is the final assertion of *Veritatis Splendor*, no. 59: "The judgment of conscience . . . formulates the proximate norm of the morality of a voluntary act, 'applying the objective law to a particular case'." *The Splendor of Truth: Veritatis Splendor, Encyclical Letter, August 6, 1993* (Washington DC: United States Catholic Conference, 1993), 61–62.

[19] This *application* cannot consist merely in a *deduction*, considering the *contingent* character of individual human acts.

[20] This is the traditional doctrine solemnly proclaimed by Vatican I (see above, n. 13).

[21] One is of course quite free to judge that even in a "context of

In the present situation of the world, one can of course no longer presume generally, at the level of a State, that the Catholic Church and its grounds for credibility are sufficiently presented to men, even in "majority" Catholic countries. The practical attitude of the Church, considering the right put forward by Vatican II, is justifiably modified. Furthermore, in today's world such civic tolerance may be based on a principle that is both more general and easier to apply, namely that some evils are to be tolerated to protect the common good.

This reference to the effective presentation of the grounds of credibility in a way that is truly accessible to the persons or groups in question was already examined in the sixteenth century, in the context of the recently discovered Americas. Here is Francisco de Vitoria's thought:

> [T]he barbarians are not bound to believe, from the first moment that the Christian faith is announced to them, in the sense of committing a mortal sin merely by not believing a simple announcement, unaccompanied by miracles or any other kind of proof or persuasion, that the true religion is Christian. . . . [I]t is not sufficiently clear to me that the Christian faith has up to now been announced and set before the barbarians in such a way as to oblige them to believe it under pain of fresh sin. By this I mean that, as explained in my second proposition, they are not bound to believe unless the faith has been set before them with persuasive probability. But I have not heard of any miracles or signs, nor of any exemplary saintliness of life sufficient to convert them. On the contrary, I hear only of provocations, savage crimes, and multitudes of unholy acts. From this, it does not appear

Christendom," such a presumption was overly systematic or lacking in nuance.

that the Christian religion has been preached to them in a sufficiently pious way to oblige their acquiescence; even though it is clear that a number of friars and other churchmen have striven industriously in this cause, by the example of their lives and the diligence of their preaching, and this would have been enough, had they not been thwarted by others with different aims.[22]

4. Complementary technical precisions

Concerning the classic doctrine

According to the lexicographical research in my work,[23] it could at first seem that "freedom of conscience" meant at the time—in the first two thirds of the nineteenth century—the freedom of acting according to one's conscience in religious matters. Some of the quoted texts do speak, with reference to "freedom of conscience," of religious opinions "believed to be in conformity with truth."[24] But other texts, which are no less numerous, mention no such thing.[25] Furthermore, the quotations of the first sort generally distinguish "freedom of conscience" from "freedom of worship," and do not mention acting "according to what one believes to be true" for the second notion.

---

[22] Francisco de Vitoria, *On the American Indians*, 2. 3–4, §§34, 38 (lecture prepared for the 1537–38 academic session, but delivered only in 1539), translated in Anthony Pagden ed., *Francisco de Vitoria. Political Writings* (Cambridge: Cambridge University Press, 1991), 269, 271.

[23] *BL*, 26–33.

[24] *BL*, 27–32, C), D), DD), G) second quotation, L) mentioning the "demands of one's conscience."

[25] *BL*. A), B), E), F), G) first quotation, H), J), K). Quotation G) [from the famous Émile Littré, *Dictionnaire de la langue française*, 1875 ed.] presents this mention in a passage drawn from vol. 3 and omits it in a passage drawn from vol. 1.

What emerges from this situation is that the mention of what is "believed to be in conformity with truth" is not an essential and commonly accepted element of the lexical description of the expression "freedom of conscience (and of worship)" at the time under discussion.

Furthermore, one must keep in mind that in the writings of many nineteenth-century authors, the word "believe," especially in such a context, may take on a purely subjective, if not affective, meaning.

It is above all by examining the documentation concerning the context and preparation of the encyclicals as well as their very text that one can be sure that it is indeed the right to the liberty of *acting as one wishes* that was then aimed at. This lexicographical research provides only a sound presumption in that direction.

As far as concerns this context, I shall merely draw attention to the text of Rozaven[26] for *Mirari Vos*, and to the first of the five propositions[27] for *Quanta Cura*.

Fr. Rozaven was one of the theologians tasked with presenting a proposal for drawing up the encyclical. In his presentation, one reads:

> *Religious Liberty.* By these words is meant the full and entire freedom of all worship in the broadest and most limitless sense. . . . By virtue of this so-called right, all governments would be under the obligation to permit the free exercise not only of all Christian sects without distinction, but also of Mohammedanism, paganism, Deism, and any other religion that an impure or insane imagination might invent, on the grounds that no government might violate the legitimate rights of individuals.

[26] *BL*, 94
[27] *BL*,184–185

The "five propositions" are an essential element of Fr. Bilio's essay. He was the main architect of the ultimate preparation of *Quanta Cura*. The first proposition to be condemned stated:

> The liberty that is termed "of worship" or "of conscience" in affairs of religion, meaning that all are free to follow any religion, even a false one, is a right proper to each man that may be impeded by neither the Church nor civil government.

In the text of the two encyclicals the link established with indifferentism or with naturalism, depending on the case, clearly demonstrates that what is envisaged is a freedom of acting as one wishes.

Concerning Dignitatis Humanæ

Some passages of the conciliar declaration would appear to have been written from the perspective of a right to act "as one wishes," and not just "according to one's conscience." The most characteristic passage is at the end of no. 2:

> Therefore, the right to religious freedom has its foundation not in the subjective disposition of the person, but in his very nature. In consequence, the right to this immunity continues to exist even in those who do not live up to their obligation of seeking the truth and adhering to it. . . .

Despite the impression this text gives at first glance, the second sentence does not assert the right to act as one wishes. The immunity in question is the right previously defined, i.e. the right to act according to one's conscience. The sentence asserts that one who does not satisfy the obligation mentioned preserves this right: that much is true. But the sentence does not assert (although it does seem to suggest it) that he who behaves in this way is always—and, as it were, unquestionably—acting according to his conscience. Nor does it say that one must necessarily and always consider him to be acting according to his conscience.

In fact, according to the first of the two quoted sentences, the purpose of the passage is to underscore the *objective character* of the right it asserts, which is therefore independent of the individual's efforts to acquire a right conscience and is not based on that potential effort. This point remains intact in the interpretation I am proposing. My interpretation is founded not only on the literal meaning of the passage, but also on the reference that the conciliar text makes, at precisely this place, to the statements of Leo XIII and Pius XII. This guarantees that it is indeed in a traditional, realist, and objective sense that the Council here speaks of "acting according to one's conscience."

Perhaps some few other passages too seem to suggest or presuppose the right to act "as one wishes." I shall here recall[28] that only the right as it is defined in *Dignitatis Humanæ* no. 2 is presented both as the direct object of conciliar teaching and as founded on Revelation. This teaching alone can lay claim to the absolute guarantee of divine assistance. That is what—and it is perfectly compatible with formerly defined doctrine, as we have seen—must serve as a norm of interpretation for the contentious passages, not the other way around.

We are here touching upon an essential point, which will surely be brought further into light during the discussions initiated by Benedict XVI's address on the hermeneutic of Vatican II. Divine assistance (in its various degrees) properly concerns the Magisterium in the exercise of its act, and not the prior discussions in which men speak

---

[28] See n. 9 above.

with no more than their own human capacities. This is why the context that bestows its meaning on a new text of the Magisterium is *more formally* made up of the body of doctrine already formally taught than by the personal orientations of the speakers during the elaboration of the documents. This, of course, does not imply that the study of preparatory documents, discussions, and the diverse drafts of the final document are of no use in understanding it. That, however, is not what sheds the ultimately decisive light. The next paragraph will illustrate this clarification.

5. Quasi-experimental observation of divine assistance

The foregoing suggests a remark. In the nineteenth century many theologians, perhaps even Gregory XVI and Pius IX, judged that man does not have a (natural) right to act in religious matters in the external and public forum if he is in error (therefore even if he is truly acting according to his conscience). This theological judgment was tempered, in practice, by the development of the theory of civil toleration with a view to the common good. Those theologians, perhaps also those popes, were therefore ready to condemn the assertion of a natural right to act according to one's conscience in religious matters. And yet, it was only the assertion of a right to the freedom of acting as one wishes (in religious matters) that was condemned.

Inversely, at Vatican II, many Fathers were most certainly partisans of the assertion of a natural right to the freedom to act as one wishes in religious matters. In fact, such was probably the case of the drafters of the text. And yet, it was only the natural right to act according to one's conscience (in religious matters) that was officially proclaimed through the declaration.

One may therefore say that in each of these two cases, what was officially taught differs from the ideas of the men most involved in drafting the texts. Perhaps even, especially in the second of the two cases, some of those men did not perceive the distance separating the assertion in the text from their own ideas. This remark is in fact an indispensable key to the hermeneutic of continuity.

It seems therefore legitimate to see in the sequence of these two episodes a tangible manifestation of the divine assistance given to the Church's infallible Magisterium.

6. Why is this important?

There are many who do not clearly perceive the reason for the importance attributed to this question of "religious liberty" since the beginning of the current crisis in the Church (the Vatican II era).

Indeed, all agree in granting that in fact, today, societies must allow civil liberty to the diverse religions ("within necessary limits"). In any event such was the position of the traditional draft originally prepared for Vatican II and presented by Cardinal Ottaviani, which appealed to the common good and tolerance.

The extreme importance of this debate, therefore, does not concern practical applications. It derives from the absolute engagement of the Church's Magisterium in one of the foundational principles involved in this matter. The matter of the infallibility of the Magisterium is here deeply involved in a particular problem of fundamental political morals.

This point has too often been overlooked. Indeed, the *Moderns* are well known for their ultra-minimalism when it comes to infallibility, and they consequently avoid invoking such a divine guarantee—even for what they are attached to. Likewise, many Traditionalists, with a view to justifying their fight against modern deviations, have found no other path than to exclude wholesale any infallibility at all from Vatican II. This is how the two tendencies have ultimately come to a tacit understanding, and the only crucial question ends up being generally ignored.

Let us then try to be precise, albeit very summarily. The fundamental principle involved is that of the "natural right of the person to civil liberty in religious matters." We have seen how Vatican II does not assert exactly what Gregory XVI and Pius IX condemned (see above, no. 2). Now I shall succinctly show that the position of Gregory XVI and Pius IX, on one hand, and that of Vatican II, on the other hand, have a *de jure* claim to infallibility.

Gregory XVI[29] condemned this principle as an "absurd and erroneous proposition," "insane," "a pernicious error": all notes that indicate the absoluteness of the condemnation. Further, in his brief of October 5, 1833 to the Bishop of Rennes,[30] Gregory XVI asserts that he was imposing nothing else (in *Mirari Vos*) than "what has been established by the tradition of the Apostles and of the Fathers": this entailed that Lammenais (who was the party concerned in the brief) had to follow the doctrine as taught "solely and *absolutely*." Lastly, in the encyclical *Singulari Nos* of June 24, 1834, Gregory XVI speaks expressly of the Catholic "teaching transmitted in Our

---

[29] *Mirari Vos*, August 15, 1832, §14. For the debate over the infallibility of the judgment expressed in *Mirari Vos*, see BL 61–63n113. The English versions of Gregory XVI, *Mirari Vos* and Pius IX, *Quanta Cura* are from Claudia Carlen, IHM, *The Papal Encyclicals*, vol. 1, *The Papal Encyclicals 1740–1878* (Raleigh: Pierian Press, 1990), 235–41 and 381–386 respectively. They are also accessible at *Papal Encyclicals Online* https://www.papalencyclicals.net/ [accessed July 17, 2024].

[30] See BL 61.

encyclical letter,"[31] particularly on "complete liberty of conscience, which is condemnable."[32]

As for Pius IX, he reasserted the condemnation issued by Gregory XVI[33] and described the condemned principle as follows: "that erroneous opinion, most fatal in its effects on the Catholic Church and the salvation of souls, called by Our Predecessor, Gregory XVI, an 'insanity'." Furthermore, in the sixth paragraph of his encyclical, Pius IX, in the name of his apostolic office, asserted the absolute bearing of his judgment upon all Catholics:

> Amidst, therefore, such great perversity of depraved opinions, *We, well remembering our Apostolic Office*, and very greatly solicitous for Our most holy Religion, for sound doctrine and the salvation of souls which is entrusted to Us by God, and (solicitous also) for the welfare of human society itself, have thought it right again to raise up Our Apostolic voice. Therefore, by Our Apostolic authority, We reprobate, proscribe, and condemn *all the singular and evil opinions and doctrines severally mentioned in this letter*, and will and command that *they be thoroughly held by all children* of the Catholic Church as *reprobated, proscribed and condemned*.

We are here presented with an absolute and repeated engagement of the papal Magisterium on a fundamental principle of morals. It is presented absolutely to the whole Church in the name of the Apostolic Office and in the name of conformity with Apostolic Tradition. The condemnation as issued does therefore constitute a point necessarily linked to Revelation and must be received by

---

[31] Viz. in *Mirari Vos.*
[32] See *BL* 68.
[33] *Quanta cura*, § 3. See *BL* 123–125.

all as definitive (see canon 750.2, along with the precisions added by the Apostolic Letter *Ad Tuendam Fidem*), since it is guaranteed by the infallibility of the divinely assisted Magisterium.[34]

Let us move on to the statement of Vatican II concerning the right to religious liberty.[35] First of all, this affirmation comes from the universal Magisterium, made up of all the bishops together with the Pope: this "subject" is indeed capable of proposing doctrine infallibly.

Next, the statement on the right to religious liberty undoubtedly constitutes a point that is *directly aimed at*—perhaps, in fact, the only one in this document. We are here dealing not merely with explanations, deductions, or illustrations, but in fact with what the Magisterium teaches primarily and of itself. This affirmation therefore has the benefit of divine assistance, which has a claim to internal adherence on the part of the faithful. It is common knowledge, however, that such internal adherence can only be probable and relative, not definitive.

There is, however, something more to be said in this specific instance. Indeed, the text goes beyond merely stating the existence of this right. The text (the Council, the universal Magisterium) "[m]oreover . . . declares that the right to religious liberty is, in truth, *based* on the very dignity of the human person, which is known both through the

---

[34] See Congregation for the Doctrine of the Faith, *Doctrinal Commentary on the Concluding Formula of the* Professio fidei (June 29, 1998), no. 8, *Acta Apostolicæ Sedis* 90 (1998): 547. English version accessible at https://www.vatican.va/roman_curia/congregations/cfaith/documents/rc_con_cfaith_doc_1998_professio-/fidei_en.html [accessed 07/30/2024].

[35] I will add that the affirmation of infallibility I am here presenting does not involve *all* of the Second Vatican Council, or *all* the Declaration *Dignitatis Humanæ*, but *only* the central assertion of no. 2 that sets forth the right to religious liberty (as defined in the same first paragraph of no. 2).

revealed *Word of God* and by reason itself." The universal Magisterium, therefore, explicitly presents its assertion as necessarily linked to ("based on") Revelation. That is why, while this passage does not include any particular formulas that allow one to speak of "solemn judgment" or "definition in an extraordinary manner," it is included in what is *presented* by the ordinary and universal Magisterium as definitive to the extent that it is necessarily linked to Revelation. *This* assertion is therefore infallibly guaranteed by divine assistance.

A fair number of "traditionalist" authors have questioned whether Vatican II ever involved infallibility. They first claimed that Vatican II was not infallible *because* it was pastoral. This manifestly confuses finality (the aims of the Council were indeed expressly pastoral) with formal cause (the Council may very well have, with a pastoral aim, infallibly asserted revealed doctrines, or doctrines linked to Revelation). Every Catholic is well aware that nothing is more important in pastoral matters than doctrinal, even dogmatic, truth presented in a spirit of charity.

Sometimes the argument takes on a different aspect. Rome, it is said, added an official "clause of non-infallibility" to the Second Vatican Council. To support this thesis, its authors invoke the speech Paul VI gave during the General Audience of January 12, 1966: "Given the Council's pastoral character, it avoided pronouncing . . . dogmas endowed with the note of infallibility." But the authentic quotation of Paul VI is this:

> Given the pastoral character of the Council, it has *avoided* pronouncing *in an extraordinary* manner dogmas endowed with the note of infallibility; but it has nevertheless endowed its teachings with the *authority of the supreme ordinary Magisterium.* This ordinary and manifestly authentic Magisterium must be received sincerely

and with docility by all the faithful, according to the Council's mind as to the *nature* and *purposes* of the individual documents.[36]

Clearly what the Council "avoided" is the involvement of the infallible Magisterium *in an extraordinary manner.* Paul VI, however, did not at all assert—and indeed the end of his text clearly implies the opposite—that the Council had *in no way* involved infallibility. Infallibility is involved to the extent that it is linked to the *supreme ordinary Magisterium.* We have precisely seen that, as far as concerns the central assertion of *Dignitatis humanæ,* the conditions for infallibility *of the ordinary supreme Magisterium*—here meaning of the *ordinary and universal Magisterium*—were in fact in play.

7. Temporary conclusion

The non-contradiction on the central point between Vatican II and earlier Catholic doctrine does not solve— far from it!—all the questions one can raise regarding *Dignitatis Humanæ* or less important teachings on the topic since the Council. It does, however, show that the orientations that Benedict XVI proposed regarding the hermeneutic of Vatican II are, in fact, applicable *to the very point that is* a priori *the most resistant to such a treatment.*

At a time when the Holy Father [Benedict XVI—*trans.*] seems committed to restoring the so-called rite of Saint Pius V to its rightful place, and may even establish the

---

[36] Paul VI, General Audience of January 12, 1966, italics mine. The whole text is available on the Vatican website (in Italian), https://www.vatican.va/content/paul-vi/it/audiences/1966/documents/hf_p-vi_aud_19660112.html [accessed July 17, 2024]. This text had already been quoted with a good commentary by Fr. Guérard des Lauriers, *Cahiers de Cassiciacum* 1 (May 1979): 15–16n8.

necessary juridical situations to put an end, at the diocesan level, to the marginalization of the faithful, both clergy and laymen, who are fully attached to this rite and to the whole spiritual and doctrinal tradition it represents[37], it would be a shame for the living forces of renewal to stand aside, while it increasingly seems that the doctrinal obstacle, so long believed to be absolute, can be overcome.

---

[37] Shortly after the publication of this article, Benedict XVI granted freedom to the traditional Mass with the motu proprio *Summorum Pontificum* of July 7, 2007 —Editor's note.

TWO

A Modest Follow-Up on Religious Liberty and Vatican II[†]

Fr. Bernard Lucien

Among the problems posed by the Vatican II declaration on Religious Liberty, Dignitatis Humanæ *(DH), there are the following: is its principal teaching infallible, or merely proposed directly by the simply authentic Magisterium? May a Catholic suspend assent to this teaching, or even refuse it, and if so, under what conditions? Some theologians, including even traditionalists, differ on the answer to the first of the two questions. The controversy between Fathers Christophe Héry[1] and Bernard Lucien provides food for thought on the second of the two questions, which is important for the attitude of the faithful to magisterial texts in general and to the status of Vatican II in particular.*

It is worth emphasizing that the question at the center of this controversy is far from exhausting the problem.

[†] Originally published in *Sedes Sapientiæ* 97 (2007), 19–39.

[1] Fr Héry is a member of the Institute of the Good Shepherd. One can only rejoice in the recent canonical erection of this institute by the Holy See as a society of apostolic life of pontifical right, and in the fact that it has been granted the exclusive use of the liturgical books in force in 1962, which constitute its proper rite.

A magisterial text includes what is taught "primarily and of itself," but also an entire 'scaffolding' of considerations and explanations.[2] *The quality of the latter influences the correct interpretation of the central teaching, and can either facilitate or compromise it.* Dignitatis Humanæ *presents significant deficiencies from this point of view, which deficiencies were immediately pointed out by members of the* Cœtus Internationalis Patrum *(which brought together the traditional-leaning Fathers at Vatican II) and are increasingly acknowledged today across a diversity of theological and ecclesial horizons.*

There should therefore be no simplistic and dialectical reading of this debate. To assert that the central teaching of Dignitatis Humanæ *is not in contradiction with the prior Magisterium in no way implies wanting to "justify the Council at any cost" or falling into some magisterial "fundamentalism." So Fr Victor-Alain Berto, Archbishop Marcel Lefebvre's peritus at the Council, while clearly asserting that "no error is formally taught" in DH, had no qualms in publicly criticizing "the doctrinal density" of this text, which is "so far beneath what one should expect from so solemn an assembly and the roughly four billion [Francs—trans.] it cost. It was a high cost for such a mountain of speeches that ended up giving birth to texts in which the turgescence of superlatives fails to mask the mediocrity of content."*[3]

---

[2] This distinction is far from being a scholastic subtlety and has many applications in the history of magisterial theology. It allows for an interpretation of Boniface VIII's highly controverted bull *Unam Sanctam* that does not fall into papal theocracy; it also preserves the substantial continuity of the Church's teaching on Church-State relations. See Charles Journet, *La Juridiction de l'Église sur la cité* (Paris: Desclée de Brouwer, 1931).

[3] Offprint, *Itinéraires* 132 (April 1969): 141.

In a recent article,[4] Fr. Christophe Héry took up the study on religious liberty I had published in *Sedes Sapientiæ*.[5]

Leaving aside anything in that text that is at some variance with basic courtesy—doubtless under the strain of passionate oratory—I shall here examine those points that are likely to be generally helpful in promoting an understanding of the question. My endeavor will be to cleave to the form of constructive controversy.

I assume that the readership is made up of Catholics: this will explain the *method* that I shall describe in the first part of this essay. Yet I am well aware that, even among those "attached to Tradition," there is sometimes a dearth of basic knowledge. For this reason, the second part, in the course of going over the difficulties Fr. Héry encountered in my presentation on religious liberty at Vatican II, will cover several points of often elementary doctrine. Brought into a synthesis, these points will doubtless shed some light for readers. Finally and unfortunately, I shall have to be a little harsh in the third part as a result of the treatment Fr. Héry reserved for the words of His Holiness Benedict XVI.

---

[4] Christophe Héry, "Vraie tolérance et fausse liberté religieuse. Le problème crucial de l'abbé B. Lucien," *Mascaret* 281 (July–August 2006): 6–7. Henceforth Héry followed by page, column, and paragraph number, e.g.: Héry, 6.2.2.

[5] Bernard Lucien, "Vatican II et 'l'herméneutique de la continuité.' Le cas crucial de la liberté religieuse," *Sedes Sapientiæ* 96 (Summer 2006): 3–22; English version, "Vatican II and the 'Hermeneutic of Continuity': The Crucial Case of Religious Liberty," above, pp. 1–22.

THE GENERAL OBLIGATIONS
OF THE CATHOLIC FAITH TOWARDS
A MAGISTERIAL TEXT

In his response to Catholic writers who claim that there is no *contradiction* between the central teaching of *Dignitatis Humanæ*[6] and the Church's doctrine as infallibly determined in the past,[7] Fr. Héry expresses a fear regarding an error in method:[8]

> Haunted as they are by a concern to preserve the Council's magisterial infallibility without harming Tradition, four [theologians] . . . have analyzed the problem that the interpretation of the conciliar declaration *Dignitatis Humanæ* raises . . ., all the while presupposing the conclusion they end up reaching, namely that *a priori* there cannot be any discontinuity between the conciliar magisterium and Tradition.

Everything here is wrong.

All of the theologians he lists started out (in different ways) convinced of the contradiction between *DH* (central teaching) and former, infallibly determined doctrine. This is well known in my own case as well as in that of Fathers de Blignières and de Saint Laumer; it was also the case for the other two, as Fr. Héry could easily find out by asking them.

---

[6] Declaration of Vatican II Council on the right to civil liberty in religious matters. This *central* teaching, the only one for which certain theologian (including myself) assert the infallible teaching of the Church, is at *Dignitatis Humanæ* 2.1. Henceforth *DH*.

[7] As it appears in the declarations of Gregory XVI (*Mirari Vos*) and Pius IX (*Quanta Cura*).

[8] Héry, 6.1.3.

The Council's infallibility is not at stake for all of them, since neither Fr. Valuet nor Fr. Harrison assert it, with the former seeming inclined to deny it.[9]

On the other hand, Fr. Héry, by his silence and his attitude, seems unaware of the requirements of the Catholic faith.

Indeed, all Catholics, by the supernatural faith with which they are imbued, have a general attitude of adherence to the teaching of the authentic Magisterium. This general attitude of adherence consists precisely in receiving the teaching of the authentic Magisterium *as it gives it to us*.

This phrase "as it gives it to us" covers a variety of cases, from teachings that involve infallibility to a mere divine assistance given to the pedagogy of the Magisterium, through merely relative engagement: that is why this *general* attitude of adherence does not exclude the concrete possibility of non-adherence in a particular case (in which infallibility is not involved). Nevertheless, for a Catholic such an instance of non-adherence is located within the *general presupposition of acceptance*.

The reason for this is quite simple and touches on a fundamental aspect of Catholicism. Divine and Catholic faith supposes (in adults) a (more or less explicit) judgment of credibility. This judgment of credibility rests on *historical* knowledge about Our Lord: His life, His teaching, and His miracles, especially His death and resurrection. And, in conjunction with this, this judgment of credibility bears upon the historically attested founding of the Church by

---

[9] For Fr. Basile Valuet, OSB, see his thesis *La Liberté religieuse et la tradition catholique* (Le Barroux: Abbaye Sainte Madeleine, 2nd ed., 1998) 38–47; for Fr. Harrison, see Brian Harrison, *Le Développement de la doctrine catholique sur la liberté religieuse* (Chémeré-le-Roi: Société Saint-Thomas d'Aquin/Bouère: Dominique Martin Morin, 1988), 10.

Our Lord for the purpose of extending His mission. The judgment of credibility cannot, however, penetrate into the details of the Church's reality and nature: faith alone permits this. Hence, supernatural faith, materially resting upon the judgement of credibility, first and necessarily adheres to God Who reveals Himself, to Our Lord, and lastly to the Church considered globally as extending the mission of the Word incarnate (the mission of teaching, sanctifying, and governing).

The differentiations within our concrete adherence to this or that act of the Church may, in the optics of faith, only be linked to differentiations pronounced by the Church herself. That is what is implied in the theological fact of global adhesion to the Church.[10]

Here now is the "methodological" application of which Fr. Héry seems unaware. Faced with a magisterial text—truly "authentic," whether it is infallible or not—every Catholic at first spontaneously (with the very spontaneity of the life of faith) adopts a habitual and global tendency towards adherence.[11] To this attitude on the part of the faithful corresponds, in any authentic magisterial statement, a key fact about its meaning: namely, the most relevant *context* of an *authentic* magisterial text, precisely

---

[10] It is the Church that tells me how to adhere to the various doctrines that she gives; therefore, in order to know according to what degree of adherence I must receive this or that doctrine, I must first adhere in a global way to the word of the Church — *Editor's note.*

[11] The term "adherence" corresponds to what is taught "first and of itself" by the Magisterium. The Catholic's *a priori* attitude towards further considerations and explanations, which may include debatable elements, will be a sincere effort to understand what is said. This *docility* does not exclude *lucidity* on the theologian's part; it presupposes it. In some cases, it may lead to the uncovering of more or less serious deficiencies, even to constructive proposals to correct what the theologian may perceive as unsound or mixed with errors (see can. 212.3).

as *authentic*, is the totality of the revealed datum and, more precisely, the totality of what the Magisterium has already determined.

This is why, even in the case of a *simply* authentic text,[12] the faithful's *a priori* attitude is one of *reception* and *comprehension* of its statements in a sense that conforms to the totality of former teaching.

Further, if a new text includes, in its actual wording, several possible interpretations (let us say two interpretations) of which one is *compatible* with former teaching and the other *contradictory* to it, it is the compatible interpretation that is the true meaning, the *magisterial and authentic* meaning, of the new document.

Such is the attitude required of every Catholic believer, be he theologian or not, cleric or not, and it is that adopted by the theologians whom Fr. Héry quotes. Such is the attitude he has forgotten: this is what prevents him from proceeding in a correct, Catholic manner in the discussion on *DH*.

Indeed—and this is my ultimate conclusion regarding this matter of method—it follows from the theological situation I have described above that if (a case that I admit as a possibility, as do most theologians) a Catholic thinks that he discerns a true *contradiction* between a new text of the authentic Magisterium (supposing it is not certainly infallible) and prior teaching, *the burden of proof rests with him.* This Catholic must be able to point to something immediately obvious or to a conclusive argument to be able to *assert*[13] the fact of the contradiction.

---

[12] As a reminder, statements of the authentic Magisterium that *are not* infallible are termed "simply" authentic.

[13] I do mean "assert," here leaving aside as off-topic the question of the instinct of faith, which keeps the Catholic from adhering to an error against the faith, even if he lacks the ability to provide an explanation.

This is what I had done—or rather, what I thought I had done—in my work on Gregory XVI, Pius IX, and Vatican II. That work, however, only was conclusive to the extent that it claimed to establish that there is no possible interpretation in favor of non-contradiction.

With God's grace, however, I have now provided a *possible* interpretation in favor of this non-contradiction; it is an interpretation that is not refuted by any of the existing works on the subject that I am aware of.

This, then, is why I must adhere (whether absolutely or relatively, depending on whether infallibility is engaged) to the central text of *DH*, even if I cannot *positively justify* this new doctrinal statement on the basis of sound theological arguments, even if I am not able to *establish positively* the continuity between this new statement and earlier statements.

Of course, what here applies to me likewise applies to any Catholic, including Fr. Héry. Yet has he not in fact brought out the *impossibility* of my conciliatory interpretation? That is what we shall examine in my second part. I do beg the reader, however, to keep in mind the methodological conclusion: given the situation, *it is up to Fr. Héry to establish rigorously the impossibility of my interpretation*, whereas all I need to do is point out its *non-impossibility*.[14]

---

[14] Given the importance of the subject, I dare hope that no one will engage in any degree of irony concerning these distinctions (burden of proof, impossible, non-impossible). They are indispensable in theology, they are absolutely classical, and anyway they are universally accepted today generally, be it in science, in logic, or in philosophy. Should someone try weaponizing derision to avoid the epistemological situation, he would be providing a sufficient reason to doubt whether he is seeking the truth.

A FEW CLARIFICATIONS
ABOUT MY INTERPRETATION
OF *DIGNITATIS HUMANÆ*

Reminder: the key distinction I have introduced

Remember that, in my view,[15] the essential difference between the right asserted by *Dignitatis Humanæ* and that condemned by Gregory XVI and Pius IX consists in the following:

- *Dignitatis Humanæ* asserts the natural right to the [external] liberty to act, in religious matters, ACCORDING TO ONE'S CONSCIENCE;

- the analysis of the texts of the two popes mentioned above show that they deny the existence of a natural right to the external liberty to act, in religious matters, AS ONE WISHES.[16]

This distinction between "acting as one wishes" and "acting according to one's conscience" is entirely elementary and well-known to all writers since the Old Testament, though it has been expressed in a diversity of ways.

In any human act, man acts *as he wishes*: this is because man is free, and every truly human act occurs under the control of the will guided by reason.

On the other hand, since the judgment of conscience applies general principles (natural and supernatural) of action to a particular case, man can:

---

[15] See "Vatican II and the 'Hermeneutic of Continuity'," 6–8.
[16] See my *Grégoire XVI, Pie IX et Vatican II. Études sur la liberté religieuse dans la doctrine catholique* (Tours: Forts dans la Foi, 1990), chapters 1 and 2.

- *follow his conscience*: I know that theft is evil, I see that this act would be theft, I do not commit this act;

- *act against his conscience*: I know that theft is evil, I know that these delicious cakes are not mine; pushed by gluttony, I devour them anyway;

- or even act *without conscience*: a man may be so accustomed to living according to his passions than he no longer even forms a judgement of conscience. The Sacred Scriptures speak in this sense of those who "drink iniquity like water" (Job 16:16), and the moralists often use the expression "a seared conscience" (1 Tim. 4:2).

The distinction I am using is therefore a distinction between a whole (of human acts) and its truly distinct parts (the three categories among human acts in relation to the judgment of conscience). This distinction is so elementary that even children perceive it (at least "according to one's conscience" vs. "against one's conscience") well before they turn seven.

Now, the *application* of this distinction to shed light on the problem of a right to civil liberty in religious matters may be *new*,[17] but this in no way constitutes a difficulty or an objection—except, that is, for such persons as harbor a *false conception of Tradition* and are suspicious of anything that does not materially and literally repeat the expressions of the past. On the contrary, in Vatican II there is obviously the acknowledgment of a *development of doctrine*

---

[17] I say "may be," since I have not done any special research on this point, which is unimportant, as I explain in the text.

on the question of religious liberty. It is therefore normal, legitimate, and *Catholic* for the theologian to endeavor to shed light on this development by means of arguments or distinctions that have not been formulated so far: otherwise, the development would already have taken place. All of this is elementary, and shows that the two unfavorable preconceptions put forward by Fr. Héry[18] ("this distinction . . . is in no way traditional" and "is founded on no magisterial authority") are off-topic and actually distract the attention of the non-expert reader from the true state of the question.

On the contrary, a Catholic approach to the situation leads me to say: if this distinction is *required* to bring out the agreement among the diverse texts of the magisterium, then it is *by that very fact* founded on the authority of the magisterium, and *substantially* traditional.

Of course, this last statement requires that the distinction I have put forth is intrinsically fit to remove the contradiction. Fr. Héry makes various objections to it, and examining these will enable us to clarify the essential question at stake.

Does the interpretation proposed by Fr. Lucien not confuse internal and external forum?

Such is the principal (and to tell the truth the only) objection in the speculative order that Fr. Héry puts forward.[19]

---

[18] Héry, 7.1.3. Fr. Héry also calls our distinction "sophisticated." If he means "complicated," I should answer that it doesn't take him much . . . and if he means "spurious," I should ask him to provide proof. Indeed, a distinction between a whole and one of its parts is a good distinction, and to say that a right bears upon only one of the parts of a set of realities is also a good distinction.

[19] He presents it in different forms; see Héry 7.2.4–5.

It is regrettable that my confrere, in formulating this most classical of objections to those proposing a civil right to act based upon the sincerity of one's conscience, did not trouble to read my explanations on the subject more carefully. They are the heart of my article[20] and, had he read them, he would not have revived—*without taking any of my arguments into account*—the difficulties my work had laid to rest.

So let us begin by recalling that Vatican II *does not base* the right to the civil liberty to act in religious matters upon the *sincerity of one's conscience*. My interpretation, of course, is in conformity with this. The determination "according to one's conscience" concerns the *object* of the right, not *its basis*.[21]

That being the case, the question that presents itself (and this is Fr. Héry's objection) is this: Can legitimate authority

---

[20] See my "Vatican II and the 'Hermeneutic of Continuity'," against which Fr. Héry states his difficulties.

[21] The Second Vatican Council strongly emphasized this distinction between object and basis in a sentence that may have caused some difficulty: "The right to religious liberty, therefore, is not based on any subjective disposition of a person, but rather in the very nature of a person. That is why the right to this immunity remains even in those who do not meet their obligation to seek the truth and embrace it" (*DH* no. 2). The significance of this precision is considerable. Indeed, if the right to religious liberty were *based* on the sincerity of one's conscience, this right would not exist among those "who do not meet their obligation etc." The Council, in this statement, strongly discarded a common mistake regarding the basis of the right. By saying that the right "remains" among those "who do not meet their obligation etc.," the Council does not aim at changing the OBJECT of the right, an object that was just defined as the liberty to act (in religious matters) ACCORDING TO ONE'S CONSCIENCE (and not at all *against* one's conscience or *without* a conscience). My study shows that there are *global societal situations* in which the mind of every man is, without any "research," presented with fundamental religious truths, so that those who disregard them cannot claim to *be acting according to their conscience*. I shall make this clear again in the remainder of the article.

discern acts that are "according to one's conscience" from those that are not? If the answer is yes, is this not attributing to authority the power of "reading consciences" and opening the way to "thought police" and totalitarianism? If the answer is no, is this not acknowledging that the proposed distinction is inoperative and therefore spurious?

These questions are quite legitimate. They were my own when I held the thesis of the contradiction between *DH* and the prior teaching. What is strange is that in formulating (in different terms) these old questions, Fr. Héry did not undertake the analysis of the article that answers them.

By acting in this way our objector strays from the normal attitude of any normal theologian when approaching a magisterial text.[22] Indeed, in order to keep up his refusal of Vatican II, Fr. Héry ought to establish not only that my distinction is *groundless*, but also that it is *strictly impossible*. He fails to do so, since he does not examine the arguments I had made for it, and he writes as though I had said nothing.

Recall that, according to my interpretation, *no power of reading consciences* is granted to legitimate authority. My study, however, shows that despite this necessary limit on authority, there are cases[23] in which the authority may *legitimately presume*[24] that when certain members

---

[22] We went over this attitude in our first epistemological part.

[23] Fr. Héry believes this restriction "destroys the scope and the basis" of my theory (Héry, 7.1.5). Such is not the case. For my theory to be operative (which is all my "theory" requires), it is sufficient for there *to be cases* in which authority is able to discern that there is no "acting according to one's conscience." Then the apparent contradiction between *DH* and the prior decrees disappears. Given the epistemological situation I had recalled in the first part (and which applies to anyone approaching the question as a Catholic), I need not establish anything more.

[24] In the sense that legitimate presumption allows a human authority to pass laws concerning the entire community in keeping with what

of the community perform this or that category of acts, they *are not acting according to their conscience*. Let me repeat: this is without reading consciences, but through an indirect conclusion based on exterior and observable objective elements.

Of course, this solution presupposes several points of philosophical and theological doctrine that could be discussed *ad infinitum*, since not all of them have reached consensus among Catholic authors. For our present purposes (a possible attitude of rejection regarding a magisterial text), however, this clause does not come into play. For, as I have explained, it is not necessary that all the elements of my solution be *positively established* for them to *bind* one who has no other way of accepting the magisterial text. It is enough for these elements not to have been *rigorously refuted*. This has not been accomplished by Fr. Héry, since he has not even begun to examine them.

Here are these principal elements:

1. the objectivity of human intelligence, which is capable of perceiving being, the true, the good, and the general principles (theoretical and practical) that concern them. This is simply the metaphysical realism of knowledge. When I say the "objectivity of intelligence," I mean this: when the intelligence has its object *seriously placed before* it, it cannot but perceive this object.

2. Furthermore, the objectivity of the grounds for credibility in the case of revealed religion, with the following precision: the Catholic faith is what causes us to hold that there are grounds for credibility *that are accessible to*

happens *ut in pluribus* ("in the majority of cases").

the understanding of all. Consequently, a man who has these grounds *seriously placed before* him, given the grace that God refuses to no one, cannot but adhere to them unless he goes against his own conscience.

3. The nature of conscience. It is not a mysterious faculty cut off from man's objective intelligence. It is an *act*, an *application in a particular case* of the *general principles* perceived by the intelligence (or by faith for the supernatural order). This understanding of what conscience is has not achieved consensus among all Catholic authors. It is, however, that of St. Thomas and, besides, as I have indicated in the former article, it has been integrated into the authentic Magisterium through the Encyclical *Veritatis Splendor* of John Paul II.[25]

4. The fact that, in conformity with their social and educable nature, human beings have the first principles of being and moral agency placed before them through the society in which they are born and grow up. One can thus objectively recognize a state of society (which can precisely be called a "Christian society") in which the general principles of religion, be it natural or revealed, are effectively placed before the intelligence of all (*ut in pluribus*, of course). And the intelligence, given its objectivity, cannot but perceive them.[26]

---

[25] See Lucien "Vatican II and the 'Hermeneutic of Continuity'," 9n18.

[26] There can, of course, be many intermediary situations: knowledge of simple natural religion, of Christianity in general, etc. We will not linger over them, since we are just stating principles here.

5. Lastly, when such a state of society exists (which is objectively observable), the authority can legitimately presume[27] that those who act *without taking into account* general religious principles *are not acting according to their conscience.*

Note that when the authority does this it *in no way reads consciences.* In such an objective situation, however, it does indirectly discern that this or that category of acts *cannot proceed from conscience,* because 1) conscience is the *application* of the general principles possessed; 2) such general principles are truly in the possession (given the state of society) of the men under consideration;[28] 3) the acts under consideration are of themselves a negation of these general principles.[29]

Such are, in summary, the elements that characterize our distinction and allow it to manifest the non-contradiction between *DH* and the prior doctrine. Fr. Héry has not examined them. He has spoken of something else, all the while exhibiting a dangerous propensity to accepting some rather modern ideas. I shall simply mention two of them.

On the one hand, in the way he radically opposes "internal forum" and "external forum," my opponent appears to indicate that he is under the influence of modern thought, which turns conscience into a world of its own absolutely independent from the life of the intelligence. On the other

---

[27] This is the simple statement that Fr. Héry is confused about.

[28] One may take as an example the acknowledgement that God exists and ought to be honored. I mean this: we are here supposing a society in which these truths are effectively societally possessed, made available to the understanding of all through the general societal milieu, education in common, etc.

[29] For instance, the distribution of pamphlets propagating atheism.

hand, in his critique of my example about just war,[30] he shows that he has left behind the thought of St. Thomas to adopt that of sixteenth-century and later authors.

Obviously, and contrary to what Fr. Héry claims, Fr. Lucien does not "derive a generality from a particular case, that of just war." Fr. Lucien, having used an analysis of principles to present a general truth, illustrated it with an example he thought—apparently, wrongly! —was well known. If the example finds disfavor, the analysis of principles remains. Fr. Héry adopts the modern theory of just war . . . that is his right. In my example I was referring to the thought of St. Thomas Aquinas, which is quite different from what developed from the sixteenth century on, in this matter as in many others concerning law and morals.[31]

My opponent, then, has provided me with an opportunity to present, in a slightly different form, the constitutive elements of an interpretation of *DH* that is in continuity with prior doctrine, and that brings out how *DH develops* implicit elements of that doctrine.

I should have liked to leave it at that. Alas, the following section and the conclusion of Fr. Héry's piece include so serious a distortion of both the thought and actual text[32] of Benedict XVI on the crucial issues of the present hour

---

[30] Héry, 7.1.6; see my "Vatican II and the 'Hermeneutic of Continuity'," 8.

[31] I recommend J.-A. Robilliard, OP, *Bulletin Thomiste* 4.6 (April–June 1935): 433–36 and Y. de La Brière, SJ, "Les trois conditions thomistes de la juste guerre et le droit des gens aujourd'hui," *Revue Thomiste* 43 (1937): 276–300 and again Robilliard, *Bulletin Thomiste* 5.7 (July–September 1938): 449–53. I had given the references to the *Bulletin Thomiste* in my earlier article. It would not have taken much to go and look them up. . . .

[32] Obviously, it is worse to distort the thought than the text. I shall here present things in the opposite order, as the *textual distortion* is the less open to debate.

that I am compelled to add a third part: did Benedict XVI condemn the assertion of *DH* on religious liberty?

BENEDICT XVI AND THE CENTRAL DECLARATION OF *DIGNITATIS HUMANÆ*

I shall therefore examine the words that Fr. Héry attributes to Benedict XVI. In my *Sedes Sapientiæ* article,[33] I had already pointed out—though without mentioning the author[34]—an important misquotation. It was an alleged assertion of Paul VI, which Fr. Héry and some of his confreres presented in a sufficiently solemn text that it was not to be forgotten within just a few months.[35] Here is what one reads in this "communiqué":[36]

> In the Council, all that is infallible is what was already held or defined as such in the Church beforehand: this non-infallibility clause is appended to the Constitution *Lumen Gentium* in the *Notifications* of November 16, 1964. It was repeated on December 7, 1965 by Pope Paul VI, then again on January 12, 1966: "Given its pastoral character, the Council avoided pronouncing dogmas endowed with the note[37] of infallibility."

To this I objected not so much a discussion on the assertion contained in the first sentence, but simply a material

---

[33] See above, "Vatican II and the 'Hermeneutic of Continuity'," 20–21

[34] In order not to seem to be making personal attacks at a time when all should endeavor to work, in truth, for the union of hearts and forces.

[35] "Communiqué des prêtres de l'église Saint-Éloi à tous les fidèles," written on or by February 19, 2006. The other authors were Fr. Philippe Laguérie, Fr. Henri Forestier, and Deacon Claude Prieur.

[36] Title III, no. 2.

[37] The text I have before me actually has "notion," manifestly a slip.

fact anyone can check: the quotation attributed to Paul VI is *false*. I went on to quote the unabridged text of Paul VI that best "corresponds" to this false quotation. Here it is now:

> Given the pastoral character of the Council, it has *avoided* pronouncing *in an extraordinary* manner dogmas endowed with the note of infallibility; but it has nevertheless endowed its teachings with the *authority of the supreme ordinary Magisterium*. This ordinary and manifestly authentic Magisterium must be received sincerely and with docility by all the faithful, according to the Council's mind as to the *nature* and *purposes* of the individual documents.[38]

[38] Paul VI, General Audience of January 12, 1966, italics mine. The whole text is available on the Vatican website (in Italian), https://www.vatican.va/content/paul-vi/it/audiences/1966/documents/hf_p-vi_aud_19660112.html [accessed July 17, 2024]. This text had already been quoted with a good commentary by Fr. Guérard des Lauriers, OP, *Cahiers de Cassiciacum* 1 (May 1979): 15–16n8. By way of forestalling chicanery, I shall specify that the text here quoted is indeed that of Paul VI on January 12, 1966, the very text to which our authors' sentence refers. This text is *different* to that of November 16, 1964 (also quoted in Basile Valuet, vol. 1, fasc. A, 30). The November 16 text, however, does not include the sentence "quoted" by our authors. As for the text of December 7, 1965, it states (see ibid. vol. II, fasc. A, 1294): "But one thing must be noted here, namely, that the teaching authority of the Church, even though not wishing to issue extraordinary dogmatic pronouncements, has made thoroughly known its authoritative teaching on a number of questions which today weigh upon man's conscience and activity," available in English on the Vatican website at https://www.vatican.va/content/paul-vi/en/speeches/1965/documents/hf_p-vi_spe_19651207_epilogo-concilio.html [accessed 08/01/2024]. There had also been a declaration of the Doctrinal Commission dated November 29, 1963, and another dated March 6, 1964. The three considerations of the Doctrinal Commission tend to assert that there would be no *infallible definition* that is not clearly declared as such. The two later interventions of Paul VI clearly indicate that sentences pronounced

Be that as it may, the error I have pointed out regarding the qualification of the Council seems minor compared to what I shall examine presently. Indeed, this time Fr. Héry claims that Benedict XVI acknowledged, and even *emphasized*, the presence of a doctrinal error in need of correction regarding the right to religious liberty proclaimed by *Dignitatis Humanæ*. Here are Fr. Héry's words:

> 4 – Finally, and above all, Fr. Lucien defends the infallibility of the conciliar definition of a "person's natural right to religious liberty" (*BL* 17) and of its metaphysical grounding in "the very dignity of the person" (*DH* no. 2), which constitutes one of the Council's most serious doctrinal errors, as Pope Benedict XVI points out.[39]

Then, upon adding the subtitle "Does Pope Benedict XVI contradict Fr. Lucien?," Fr. Héry goes on:

> Indeed, with a view to correcting this error in his December 22, 2005 address, the Holy Father castigates this theory: "Religious freedom . . . is raised inappropriately to the metaphysical level and is thus stripped of its true meaning."

Here our author launches into various comments that I shall leave aside for the time being. Indeed, it is more urgent to go straight to the source, i.e., to read the papal text supposedly quoted by our opponent:[40]

---

in an *extraordinary mode* are what was avoided. This is entirely different from our authors' claim.

[39] Héry, 7.1–2.

[40] Benedict XVI, Address to the Roman Curia Offering Them his Christmas Greetings *Expergiscere Homo* (December 22, 2005), *AAS* 98 (2006): 50. English version accessible at https://www.vatican.va/content/benedict-xvi/en/speeches/2005/december/documents/

Basic decisions, therefore, continue to be well-grounded, whereas the way they are applied to new contexts can change. Thus, for example, IF religious freedom were to be considered an EXPRESSION OF THE HUMAN INABILITY TO DISCOVER THE TRUTH and thus become a *canonization of relativism*, THEN this social and historical necessity *would be raised inappropriately to the metaphysical level* and thus stripped of its true meaning. Consequently, it cannot be accepted by those who believe that the human person is capable of knowing the truth about God and, on the basis of the inner dignity of the truth, is bound to this knowledge.

The Holy Father clearly explains that, "if" religious liberty is considered as "an expression of the human inability to discover the truth," "then . . . [it] is raised inappropriately to the metaphysical level and thus stripped of its true meaning." Fr. Héry, however, has the Holy Father say without qualification that: "Religious freedom . . . is raised inappropriately to the metaphysical level and thus stripped of its true meaning," and further claims that this *absolute* assertion is, in the very text of the pope, aimed at the central teaching of *DH*. According to Fr. Héry, the Holy Father is supposed to have *emphasized* that this is one of Vatican II's most serious errors, and also to have *castigated* this serious error!

On the contrary, of course, Benedict XVI goes on to explain in the very next part of his text that the error he has just mentioned ("if religious freedom . . .") is quite different from the teaching of the Council:

hf_ben_xvi_spe_20051222_roman-curia.html [accessed 08/01/2024]. Italics and small caps mine.

It is *quite different*, on the other hand, to perceive religious freedom as a need that derives from human coexistence, OR INDEED, as an intrinsic consequence of the truth that cannot be externally imposed but that the person must adopt only through the process of conviction.

The Second Vatican Council, recognizing and making its own an essential principle of the modern State[41] with the Decree on Religious Freedom, has recovered the deepest patrimony of the Church.[42]

Without going into a detailed analysis of the Holy Father's words, it is clearly observable that Benedict XVI here expresses his full agreement with the Vatican II definition. Likewise, it is clear that the interpretation I have given of the Vatican II text is fully consonant with the Holy Father's clarification. Consider:

1. The basic mistake, according to Benedict XVI, would be to deny *man's ability to reach the truth in religious matters.* Contrariwise, my interpretation involves as its basic and fully explicit element *the assertion of this capacity.*[43]

2. My interpretation brings to light how liberty in religious matters is both a "social necessity," an "historical necessity," and "indeed" a consequence of the "inner dignity of the

---

[41] I would be a little more nuanced about this last assertion.

[42] Benedict XVI, Address to the Roman Curia (December 22, 2005).

[43] Whereas the Vatican II text, *without denying* this capacity, and even clearly presupposing it, does not insist on it: I have, then, contributed a constructive clarification, which is in line with the present Holy Father's thinking [viz. Benedict XVI's—trans.].

truth,"[44] which truth "the person must adopt only through the process of conviction." Indeed, I insisted that the right to religious liberty did not entail the right of not being prevented from attacking religious truth *as effectively possessed* in general by the members of society [this is what corresponds to the dignity of the truth]. On the other hand, a religious truth that is not yet socially possessed cannot [here is the "social necessity" aspect] be directly opposed to the right not to be impeded from acting according to one's conscience. Lastly, I had emphasized that there is a great diversity of states of society through time and space in relation to this possession of religious truth [hence the "historical necessity" aspect].

Far from presenting a *contradiction*, therefore, Benedict's address actually presents itself as a strong *encouragement* for the interpretation of *Dignitatis Humanæ* I have proposed. The fact remains that the quotation of the Holy Father's text as presented by Fr. Héry is gravely erroneous, and that his commentary on the Pope's thought, resting as it does on this inexact basis, has led him to make the pope say the opposite of what he actually asserts. Clearly, the issue at stake is important and quite naturally calls for rectification. On this point as also with respect to the qualitative assessment of conciliar texts, a rigorous analysis of the texts is imperative in order to make credible a "serious and constructive critique" of Vatican II—which is as relevant as ever.

---

[44] This is the aspect under which one may uncover the metaphysical basis proper to the right to liberty in religious matters as asserted by Vatican II.

THREE

In Its Definition of Religious Liberty, Did Vatican II Contradict Prior Magisterium? A Solution Proposed by Fr. Lucien[†]

Fr. Antoine-Marie de Araujo, FSVF

Vatican II's declaration Dignitatis Humanæ *(DH) on religious liberty occasioned, and continues to occasion, impassioned reactions. In 1987, after in-depth research, some theologians of the Fraternity of Saint Vincent Ferrer reached the following nuanced conclusion:*

> *One may then say that the declaration is weak, equivocal, dangerous, yet not erroneous in its main teaching.[1] It is weak in its considerations: some are highly conditioned by their historical and cultural context as well as by a fairly unrealistic view of things that forgets the concrete conditions of the exercise of freedom as weakened by sin and also forgets the perversity of some of the forces*

[†] An earlier version of this article was published in *Sedes Sapientiæ* 147 (March 2019).

[1] This teaching alone is proposed with authority, *auctoritative.* "It must be clear that the argumentation is not proposed with authority," explained the Relator, *Acta Synodalia* IV, VI, 735.

before which the weak are defenseless. It is equivocal in several of its expressions; so much so that, despite the Relator's explanations,[2] it is invoked to justify the emancipation of theologians from the Magisterium. It is especially dangerous because its omissions expose it to indifferentist interpretations. In its central assertion, however, namely the right to immunity from coercion within the limits of a just public order in religious matters (DH no. 2), Dignitatis Humanæ does not contradict the prior Magisterium and even presents a homogeneous development of the doctrine on social order (Letter of the Société Saint-Thomas-d'Aquin, December 1987).

Taking a different approach, Fr. Bernard Lucien reached an analogous result in 1992: one can resolve the apparent contradiction between DH *and the prior Magisterium. Accepting the central teaching of a document in no way entails denying its ambiguities and deficiencies. Less yet does it amount to "justifying the Council at any cost." If a text actually contradicts an infallible teaching of the Church, there is nothing to be done to justify it. Conversely, however, if this contradiction can be resolved, the deficiencies in the text do not justify rejecting it. Furthermore, the clarifications that the Magisterium has provided in the* Catechism of the Catholic Church, *which resolve certain ambiguities, clearly support continuity.[3]*

This issue still presents difficulties for some Catholics, and is a stumbling block for the Society of Saint Pius X. This is why our review is tackling this subject again.

—The Editors, *Sedes Sapientiæ*, March 2019.

---

[2] *Acta Synodalia* IV, I, 185; IV, VI, 770.

[3] See D.-M. de Saint Laumer, "Le Catéchisme et la liberté religieuse," *Sedes Sapientiæ* 43 (December 1993): 28–34.

This presentation aims at making known the works of Fr. Bernard Lucien on religious liberty.[4] Their thesis is this: despite appearances, the religious liberty defined by Vatican II's declaration *Dignitatis Humanæ* is not in contradiction with the Church's prior doctrine and praxis.

First, I shall present the problem along with the solution that Fr. Lucien proposes. In order to show its relevance, I shall apply this solution to the particular case of a Catholic society. In doing so I shall attempt to show how, *in such a case*, the public exercise of non-Catholic religions may legitimately be impeded. Then I shall have to explain where this appearance of contradiction between Vatican II and the prior Magisterium comes from. I shall draw attention to an ambiguity within the text of *Dignitatis Humanæ*: the expression "acting according to one's conscience" changes meaning depending on whether one recognizes the human mind's capacity to know exterior reality (i.e., realism) or one does not (subjectivism). Next, since the traditional reading here proposed may seem arbitrary to some, I shall show that *Dignitatis Humanæ* refers to a text by Leo XIII which contains the seeds of the distinction that Fr. Lucien brings out. Several texts of the pre-conciliar Magisterium will be quoted that are along the same lines. Lastly, in a response to objections, we shall also study a few historical examples.

---

[4] Bernard Lucien, "Vatican II et 'l'herméneutique de la continuité': le cas crucial de la liberté religieuse," *Sedes Sapientiæ* 96 (2006): 3–22; English version: "Vatican II and the "Hermeneutic of Continuity": The Crucial Case of Religious Liberty," above, 1–22. Idem, "Petite suite sur la liberté religieuse et Vatican II," *Sedes Sapientiæ* 97 (2007): 19–39. English version: "A Modest Follow-Up on Religious Liberty and Vatican II," above, 23–45.

A. THE PROBLEM, AND A SOLUTION PROPOSED BY FR. LUCIEN

I. STATING THE PROBLEM

Any Catholic who reads the declaration *Dignitatis Humanæ* (*DH*) can easily wonder whether the Church has made a 180-degree turn and whether her Magisterium has been the author of a contradiction. Let us compare the conciliar text with the prior Magisterium.

Vatican II, *Dignitatis Humanæ* (December 7, 1965) no. 2.1:	Pius IX, *Quanta Cura* (December 8, 1864) no. 3 (following Gregory XVI, *Mirari Vos*, no. 14):[5]
This Vatican Council declares that a human person has a right to religious liberty. This type of liberty consists in the fact that, within necessary limits, all men need to be immune from coercion, whether deriving from individuals, social groups, or any human authority, in any matter of religion, in such a way that *no one is either forced to act against his conscience, or impeded from acting in accordance with his conscience*, regardless of whether he is acting in private or in public, alone or in association with others. Moreover it declares that the right to religious liberty is, in truth, based on the very dignity of the human person,	And, against the doctrine of Scripture, of the Church, and of the Holy Fathers, they do not hesitate to assert that "that is the best condition of civil society, *in which no duty is recognized, as attached to the civil power, of restraining by enacted penalties, offenders against the Catholic religion, except so far as public peace may require.*" From which totally false idea of social government they do not fear to foster that erroneous opinion, most fatal in its effects on the Catholic Church and the salvation of souls, called by Our Predecessor, Gregory XVI, an "insanity," viz.,

---

[5] Pius IX, Encyclical *Quanta Cura* (December 8, 1864), *Acta Sanctæ Sedis* 3 (1867): 162. English version Claudia Carlen, IHM, *The Papal Encyclicals*, vol. 1, *The Papal Encyclicals, 1740–1878* (Raleigh: Pierian Press, 1990), 382.

which is known both through the revealed Word of God and by reason itself.* This right of the human person to religious liberty should be recognized in the juridical structure of a society in such a way that it finds expression as a civil right.

* See John XXIII, Encyclical *Pacem in Terris* (April 11, 1963), *AAS* 55 (1963): 260–261; Pius XII, Radio message (December 24, 1942), *AAS* 35 (1943): 19; Pius XI, Encyclical *Mit Brennender Sorge* (March 14, 1937), *AAS* 29 (1937): 160; Leo XIII, Encyclical *Libertas Præstantissimum* (June 20, 1888).

that *"liberty of conscience and worship is each man's personal right*, which ought to be legally proclaimed and asserted in every rightly constituted society; and that a right resides in the citizens to an absolute liberty, which should be restrained by no authority whether ecclesiastical or civil, whereby they may be able openly and publicly to manifest and declare *any of their ideas whatever*, either by word of mouth, by the press, or in any other way."

Fr. Lucien summarized the problem as follows: "According to Vatican II, man has a natural right to act freely (i.e., free from human constraint) in the religious sphere, whereas Gregory XVI and Pius IX denied the existence of such a natural right." There is a contradiction if what one teaches and the others condemn *is the same thing*. If it is not the same thing, the contradiction vanishes.

II. FR. LUCIEN'S THESIS: WHAT VATICAN II TEACHES AND WHAT PIUS IX AND GREGORY XVI CONDEMNED *ARE NOT THE SAME THING*

According to Fr. Lucien, there is an essential difference between the right asserted by *DH* and that condemned by Gregory XVI and Pius IX. It consists in this:

- *Dignitatis Humanæ* affirms the natural right to the [external] liberty to act, in religious matters, ACCORDING TO ONE'S CONSCIENCE;

- · the two popes mentioned above deny the existence of a natural right to the external liberty to act, in religious matters, AS ONE WISHES.

Since these are two different things, the Church can assert the former and condemn the latter without contradiction.

III. WHAT PIUS IX AND GREGORY XVI CONDEMNED

Fr. Lucien provided a detailed analysis of the judgments of Gregory XVI and Pius IX;[6] The reader is referred to it. His main conclusions may be summarized as follows:

- Gregory XVI, when he condemned "that absurd and erroneous proposition, or rather that insanity, which claims that liberty of conscience must be maintained for everyone" (*Mirari Vos*, no. 14), condemned the very system of civil liberty in religious matters. And this system of civil liberty is rejected because it formally includes the liberty of religious error, of false religions. In rejecting this false principle, Gregory XVI denies that there is an absolute requirement, a natural right (independently from circumstantial considerations) to be granted such a liberty in religious matters.[7]

- Blessed Pius IX, in the text quoted above, follows and completes the condemnation of Gregory XVI. He denies the existence of a

[6] Bernard Lucien, *Grégoire XVI, Pie IX et Vatican II: Études sur la liberté religieuse dans la doctrine catholique* (Tours: Forts dans la foi, 1990), chapters 1 and 2.

[7] Lucien, *Grégoire XVI*, 119–20.

fundamental human right termed "liberty of conscience and worship." This civil liberty has as its object citizens' public manifestation of "any of their ideas whatever": it is, then, a liberty that encompasses the entire field of voluntary action in religious matters. Whatever ideas one wishes, one has the right, "restrained by no authority whether ecclesiastical or civil," to "be able openly and publicly to manifest and declare" them. This concerns "the religious sphere in its entirety: individual and collective activities, acts of worship and the spread of ideas, even in public, through various means.[8]

Pius IX and Gregory XVI deny that liberty applies to the totality of all religious human acts on the sole grounds that they are religious. These popes condemn an alleged natural right to the external liberty to act, in religious matters, *as one wishes*.

IV. WHY THIS IS NOT THE SAME THINGS AS WHAT VATICAN II TEACHES

As traditional Catholic moral theology teaches, all that a man wishes is not necessarily in conformity with his conscience. Often (namely by sinning) man acts voluntarily and freely, but not acting according to his conscience. Fr. Lucien explains:

This distinction between "acting as one wishes" and "acting according to one's conscience" is entirely elementary and well-known to all writers since the Old

---

[8] Lucien, *Grégoire XVI*, 149.

Testament, though it has been expressed in a diversity of ways.

In any human act, man acts *as he wishes*: this is because man is free, and every truly human act occurs under the control of the will guided by reason.

On the other hand, since the judgment of conscience applies general principles (natural and supernatural) of action to a particular case, man can:

- *follow his conscience*: I know that theft is evil, I see that this act would be theft, I do not commit that act;

- *act against his conscience*: I know that theft is evil, I know that these delicious cakes are not mine; urged by gluttony, I devour them anyway;

- or even act *without conscience*: a man may be so accustomed to living according to his passions than he no longer even forms a judgement of conscience.

Man acts as he wishes
(=willingly)

according to his conscience	against his conscience	without conscience

It belongs to man's dignity to follow the duty that his conscience dictates. He who is in conformity with his conscience has more dignity than he who is not. How does this distinction allow for the traditional meaning of religious liberty? May I be permitted a somewhat trivial comparison:

Jules, aged seventeen, has been invited to a birthday party by his neighbors and asks his parents for permission to come home late. If his parents say (1): "Come home any time you wish," they are not at all saying the same as (2): "Come home at a reasonable hour." In the first case (1), they are giving him a limitless liberty to come home at any time at all. If Jules comes home at dawn, his parents have no right legitimately to punish him. In the second case (2), they do not grant him a total liberty, but a liberty limited to what is reasonable, although they are relying on the young man's judgment. If the latter has been brought up correctly, he knows that the time to come home ought not to go past a certain limit. If Jules came home at an objectively late hour (say 5:00 A.M.), his parents might legitimately punish him, even if he claimed that, in his view, 5:00 A.M. is a reasonable time to come home.

Likewise, Vatican II did not say that, in religious matters, man has a right to do what he pleases, but only that he has the right to act according to his conscience, that is, according to what he knows to be reasonable. Now any reasonable person considers that certain religious acts at least are not reasonable: therefore, if he performs them, he is not following his conscience. For instance, if a Christian blasphemes, he is acting voluntarily, but not according to his conscience. Such an act is not protected by religious liberty, which protects only acts performed according to one's conscience.

In this understanding, religious liberty turns out to be far more restrictive than "an absolute liberty, which should be *restrained by no authority* whether ecclesiastical or civil, whereby they may be able openly and publicly to manifest and declare *any of their ideas whatever*, either by word of mouth, by the press, or *in any other way*," the liberty condemned by Pius IX and Gregory XVI (see above; my emphases). This essential difference is reflected in societal terms, as I shall now try to show.

B. PROOF: RELIGIOUS LIBERTY DOES NOT PREVENT A CATHOLIC SOCIETY FROM IMPEDING THE PUBLIC EXERCISE OF FALSE RELIGIONS AS SUCH.

- According to *DH* no. 2.1, the human person has a right to religious liberty, both in private and in public, alone or with others. This is a right not to be forced to act against one's conscience, or not to be impeded from acting according to one's conscience, within due limits,[9] in religious matters.

- Now, in a Catholic society, the authorities may *legitimately presume* that public acts against the Catholic religion are acts contrary to conscience (for example, formal sins of heresy, schism, infidelity, blasphemy, sacrilege, etc.).

- Therefore, religious liberty does not protect these acts.

Therefore, according to *DH*, a Catholic society may legitimately impede the public exercise of religious error as such.

Here is how the minor premise is established: *in a Catholic society, the authorities may legitimately presume that public acts against the Catholic religion are acts against conscience.* The truth of Catholicism (which

---

[9] This study leaves aside the question of "due limits."

possesses objective signs of credibility that are of themselves accessible to the understanding of all) constitutes an objective fact. In a Catholic society, this truth is knowable and supposed to be known to all. True religion, at least in its essential dogmas and laws, is a matter of public knowledge. Let us suppose an individual speaks out or acts against this Catholic religion. It may legitimately be *presumed* that he is not acting according to his conscience, but rather against the judgment of his conscience. If the public authorities impede this act, the person in question cannot invoke religious liberty against the authorities' intervention.

I am not saying that civil authorities have the right to impede any act a person may commit against his conscience. State intervention must be as limited as possible and must have a just motive. But, if need be, religious liberty does not prevent the authorities from intervening.[10]

C. WHY IT *SEEMS* THAT WHAT VATICAN II TEACHES AND WHAT PIUS IX AND GREGORY XVI CONDEMNED ARE THE SAME THING.

I. The expression "acting according to one's conscience" is ambiguous

"Acting according to one's conscience" does not have the same meaning depending on whether one grants the human mind the ability to know external reality (realism) or one refuses it (subjectivism).

---

[10] I shall add that considerations based on the common good may impose upon the authorities a just toleration that goes far beyond what is required by the "right to religious liberty."

a) What is "acting according to one's conscience," from the Church's realist point of view?

We follow the common doctor of the Church, Saint Thomas Aquinas:[11]

> Properly speaking, conscience is not a power, but an act. . . .
>
> For conscience is said to witness, to bind, or incite, and also to accuse, torment, or rebuke. And all these follow the application of knowledge or science to what we do: which application is made in three ways. One way in so far as we recognize that we have done or not done something; "Thy conscience knoweth that thou hast often spoken evil of others" (Ecclesiastes 7:23), and according to this, conscience is said to witness. In another way, so far as through the conscience we judge that something should be done or not done; and in this sense, conscience is said to incite or to bind. In the third way, so far as by conscience we judge that something done is well done or ill done, and in this sense conscience is said to excuse, accuse, or torment. Now, it is clear that all these things follow the actual application of knowledge to what we do.

Here Saint Thomas distinguishes: 1) *psychological* conscience, by which one is "conscious" of what he does; 2) and 3) *moral* conscience, by which he morally judges an act he has performed or is considering performing. We are here interested in the moral conscience, since religious liberty concerns man's moral action. St. Thomas defines

---

[11] Thomas Aquinas, *Summa Theologiæ*, I, q. 79, art. 13, resp. English translation: St. Thomas Aquinas, *Summa Theologica: First Complete American Edition*, trans. Fathers of the English Dominican Province (New York: Benziger Bros, 1947), 1.408. Hereafter *ST*.

it as the act by which we apply our knowledge of good and evil to our action.

Let us return to the example provided by Fr. Lucien. I have, within my reason, some knowledge: I *know* that theft is evil. I have yet to act. My reason applies this knowledge to a particular case here and now: I see that this act (taking the delicious cakes that are not mine) would be theft. At that moment, my will may choose to *follow* or not the duty that conscience indicates:

- either by *following my conscience*: I do not commit the act;

- or by *acting against my conscience*: urged by gluttony, I nevertheless devour the cakes.

Conscience alone allows us to determine the right conduct here and now. That is why St. Thomas insists on the fact that we must always follow our conscience. It is always a sin to act against one's conscience, even when it is objectively in error: "absolutely speaking, every will at variance with reason [i.e., conscience], whether right or erring, is always evil."[12]

Moral conscience is the application of knowledge to our acts through reason. But what is the force of this knowledge in religious matters? Is it not a pure subjective opinion?

Human intelligence is capable of objective and certain knowledge, including in religious matters.

The Church teaches that our mind reaches exterior reality, from which it can arrive at an objective and certain knowledge not only in those fields that Moderns call "exact sciences," but also in metaphysics, morals, and religion.[13]

---

[12] *ST* I–II, q. 19, a. 5, resp.

[13] The type of certitude varies according to the subject under review. Metaphysical and logical certainty, to which mathematical certainty

Let us quote, for example, the *Antimodernist Oath* instituted by Pius X:[14]

> And first of all, I profess that God, the beginning and end of all things, can be known with certainty and, indeed, also demonstrated through the natural light of reason from "the things that have been made" [Rom. 1:20], namely, from the visible works of creation, as the cause from its effects, and that, therefore, his existence can also be demonstrated:

> Secondly, I accept and recognize the external proofs of revelation, that is to say, the divine works, mainly the miracles and prophecies, as sure signs of the divine origin of the Christian religion, and I hold that they are well adapted to the understanding of all ages and of all men, even those of the present time.

Pius XII repeated the *objectivity* of moral norms on several occasions. One may refer to his *Radio Message to the Participants of the Seventh International Congress of Catholic Physicians*, on September 11, 1956 (my emphasis):

> Morality has as its goal the determination of the internal and external conscious attitude of man towards the great obligations which are the consequences of the essential

---

can be assimilated, outstrips that of the physical sciences, not to mention that of the so-called human sciences. At the practical level of action, there exists moral certainty, which suffices for prudent action.

[14] Heinrich Denzinger and Peter Hünermann, *Compendium of Creeds, Definitions, and Declarations on Matters of Faith and Morals*, 43rd ed. Robert Fastiggi and Anne Englund Nash (San Francisco: Ignatius Press, 2012), 3538–39 (henceforth *DzH*). See also Vatican I, *Dei Filius* chap. 3; Vatican II, *Gaudium et Spes*, no. 15; Paul VI, *Solemni Hac Liturgia (Credo of the People of God)* (June 30, 1968); John Paul II, *Fides et Ratio*, nos. 22 and 83.

conditions of human nature: obligations towards God and religion, obligations in justice towards oneself and toward one's neighbor, which means toward individuals, groups and community organizations, and obligations in the almost unlimited realm of material things.

Morality imposes the duty of regulating actions according to the aforesaid obligations on the conscience of every man, whether he is a doctor or a soldier, a scholar or a man of action.

This supposes that every man knows these obligations, or can know them if he does not know them already.

It therefore follows that *if a moral decision must be made by a man, the decision does not depend on his pleasure or his caprice, but is inspired by objective criteria.*

This is what brings forth the spontaneous question "Why?" from a man who is conscientious about himself. He wants to know the objective standards of what he proposes to do.[15]

The Holy Office Instruction of February 2, 1956, which refers to Saint Thomas (though without naming him), is just as precise. Man's ultimate decision about what he must do is,

---

[15] French original: Pius XII, *Nuntius Radiophonicus Iis Qui Interfuerunt Conventui VII Internationali Medicorum Catholicorum in Urbe Capite Hollandiæ ab 'Association Internationale des Médecins Catholiques' Indicto* (September 11, 1956), *Acta Apostolicæ Sedis* 48 (1956): 680–81. English version: "Pope's Talk to Doctors on Moral Standards for Medicine," *The Catholic Advocate* 5.47 (November 24, 1956): 9, accessible online at *The Catholic News Archive*.

as the objective ethics handed down by authors of great weight teaches, the application of the objective law to a particular case which at the same time takes into account and weighs, according to the rules of prudence, the particular circumstances of the "situation." . . . [T]his judgment is . . . measured . . . by [an] objective norm situated outside man and independent of his subjective persuasion.[16]

There exist norms of reality outside of the mind, in the known *object*. They are *objective*, independent from the *subject* who is considering them, and therefore universally valid. The conscience does not create moral norms; it receives them from the external reality and applies them to the action it is considering.

CONSEQUENCES

- Exterior reality is the object of human intelligence, which is capable of perceiving being, the true, the good, and the general principles (theoretical and practical) that concern them. When the intelligence is *seriously placed before* its object, it cannot but perceive it.[17]

- When, therefore, in a given society, certain truths are available to all, one may legitimately presume that the conscience of all the members of that society is informed of those truths.

- That a law is known to all allows, at least in certain cases, for a legitimate judgment about

---

[16] *DzH* 3918.
[17] Lucien, "Modest Follow-up," 36.

someone indirectly, based on his exterior actions. For instance, the judge may judge, in all prudence, that a thief has acted against his conscience, since everybody knows that one ought not to steal.

• Since Catholicism comes with proofs that are accessible to all, it is objectively credible to a far greater extent than any false belief. Now once truth is known it is binding in conscience, as *DH* no. 1 teaches: "all men are bound, especially in matters which concern God and His Church, to seek the truth; to embrace it, when known by them; and to safeguard it." Objectively, therefore, Catholicism is more binding in conscience than are other religions. In this respect, one can quote Vatican I:

[F]or *to the Catholic Church alone* belong all those many and admirable tokens which have been divinely established for the evident credibility of the Christian faith. . . . And its testimony is efficaciously supported by a power from on high. For our most merciful Lord gives his grace to stir up and to aid those who are astray, that they may come to a knowledge of the truth; and to those whom he has brought out of darkness into his own admirable light he gives his grace to strengthen them to persevere in that light, deserting none who desert not him. Therefore, there is no parity between the condition of those who have adhered to the Catholic truth by the heavenly gift of faith, and of those who, led by human opinions, follow a false religion; for *those who have received the faith under the magisterium of the Church can never have any just cause for changing or doubting that faith.*[18]

Under the conditions outlined above, one may presume that one who abandons or doubts the Catholic faith does not act according to his conscience.

b) What does "acting according to one's conscience" mean in modern thought?

Under the influence of Descartes and Kant especially, Moderns have become *subjectivists,* as Leo XIII lamented in his encyclical *Depuis le Jour* (September 8, 1899), no. 15:

> We are profoundly grieved to learn that for some years past some Catholics have felt at liberty to follow in the wake of a philosophy which under the specious pretext of freeing human reason from all ideas and from all illusions, *denies it the right of affirming anything beyond its own operations, thus sacrificing to a radical subjectivism* all the certainties which traditional metaphysics, consecrated by the authority of the strongest thinkers, laid down as the necessary and unshakable foundations for the demonstration of the existence of God, the spirituality and immortality of the soul, and the objective reality of the exterior world.[19]

---

[18] Vatican I, Dogmatic Constitution *Dei Filius*, chap. 3. English translation: Archbishop Henry Edward Manning, *Petri Privilegium* (London: Longmans, Green and Co., 1871), 247.

[19] Leo XIII, Encyclical *Depuis le Jour* (September 8, 1899), *Acta Sanctæ Sedis* 32 (1899–1900): 199. English version Carlen, *Papal Encyclicals*, 2.458. Accessible at https://www.papalencyclicals.net/leo13/l13depui. htm [accessed 08/13/2024].

By eliminating "traditional metaphysics" (especially that of Aristotle and Saint Thomas), which allows for the rational study of the content of revelation, subjectivism divorces faith from reason. Faith becomes the domain of the irrational, of the subjective. In religious matters, there is no more objectivity. This error has repercussions in morals. Under the pontificate of Pius XII, on February 2, 1956, the Holy Office condemned "situation ethics":

> The authors who follow this system hold that the *decisive and ultimate norm of conduct is not the objective right order, determined by the law of nature and known with certainty from that law*, but a certain *intimate* judgement and light of the mind of each individual, by means of which, in the concrete situation in which he is placed, he learns what he ought to do.

> And so, according to them, this ultimate decision a man makes is not, as the objective ethics handed down by authors of great weight teaches, the application of the objective law to a particular case, which at the same time takes into account in ways according to the rules of prudence the particular circumstances of the "situation," but that immediate, internal light and judgement. Ultimately, at least in many matters, this judgement is not measured, must not and cannot be measured, as regards its objective rectitude and truth, by any objective norm situated outside man and independent of his subjective persuasion, but is entirely self-sufficient. . . .

> Having accepted these principles and put them into practice, they assert and teach that men are preserved or easily liberated from many otherwise insoluble ethical conflicts when each one judges in his own conscience, not primarily according to objective laws, but by means of

that internal, individual light based on personal intuition, what he must do in a concrete situation.[20]

One can here see how such an expression as "acting according to one's conscience" is distorted once certain presuppositions are granted. Denying that the intelligence is subject to exterior realities and its laws turns conscience into the creator of its own moral norms. Now if conscience can consider any action good, then there is *practically no difference between acting according to one's conscience and acting as one wishes.*

CONSEQUENCES OF SUBJECTIVISM

1. All subjective convictions are, as such, equal (relativism).

Subjectivism leads to relativism. "Everyone has *his own* truth." Ideas most contrary to reason, idolatry, witchcraft, satanism, racist theories, pedophilia, anti-human environmentalism, etc., can equally be believed and adopted with a good conscience.[21]

2. It becomes impossible to know whether someone else is acting according to his conscience or not.

God alone reads consciences *directly.* One man judges another indirectly. For this, there have to be objective norms and *facts* known to all. Saying: "Peter stole this hat" presupposes that Peter knows the moral law (one ought not to steal) and the fact (this hat does not belong to him). Since these truths are objective, one legitimately presumes that they inform Peter's conscience. If, however, everyone determines *his own* truth, then I cannot presume

---

[20] *Instruction of the Holy Office* (February 2, 1956), DzH 3918–20.
[21] Relativism thus demeans man's dignity by making him blind and irresponsible.

that Peter knows what I know. I therefore cannot know whether he is acting according to his conscience.

3. *Religious truth cannot be a common good (religious liberalism)*.

According to relativism, morals, religion, and philosophy belong to the domain of the subjective. Now what is subjective is not communicable as such. *My* subjective truth cannot be valid for anyone else. Religious truth is therefore not a common good to be shared, cultivated, or defended. It does not matter if one is wrong on this issue. Religious error harms neither one's neighbor nor the community.[22] At the practical level, relativism leads to *religious liberalism*: everyone must be granted the maximum in religious matters. The United Nations' 1948 *Universal Declaration of Human Rights* says as much:[23]

> Everyone has the right to freedom of thought, conscience and religion; this right includes freedom to change his religion or belief, and freedom, either alone or in community with others and in public or private, to manifest his religion or belief in teaching, practice, worship and observance.

According to the advocates of religious liberalism, the only limit to this freedom is respect for a minimum level of public peace: "[T]hat is the best condition of civil society, in which no duty is recognized, as attached to the

---

[22] Here again Moderns are unaware of one of man's deepest aspirations. As a social animal, he desires not only to know the truth, but also to share it. He needs to share in the truth with his fellow men. Any society supposes that its members share at least some basic truths.

[23] Accessible at https://www.un.org/en/about-us/universal-declaration-of-human-rights [accessed 08/13/2024]. It is fair to say, however, that at the time, the drafters of this declaration were not entirely committed to liberalism and relativism, and that they recognized an objective moral order (—eds.).

civil power, of restraining by enacted penalties, offenders against the Catholic religion, except so far as public peace may require." In *Quanta Cura*, no. 3, Pius declares this proposition, which recognizes to the civil power the right to defend the Catholic religion only to avoid civil unrest and not for itself (since it is the true religion) to be "totally false." Ultimately, this proposition denies that the civil government can be entrusted with the function of secular arm in favor of the Catholic religion.

c) What this overview shows

- According to modern subjectivism, conscience is autonomous from objective reality and the creator of its own norms. So, in practice, the right to act according to one's conscience means the right to act *as one wishes*.

- According to realism as defended by the Catholic Church, to act according to one's conscience means to act according to objective criteria. The right to act according to conscience is only a right to act according to the elements of judgment that are objectively available to one's conscience. It is not a right to act against truths known and recognized by all.

II. HOW CAN ONE KNOW THAT THE COUNCIL DOES NOT MEAN THE EXPRESSION "TO ACT ACCORDING TO ONE'S CONSCIENCE" IN A RELATIVISTIC SENSE?

Let us quote Bishop De Smedt, Relator of the schema on religious liberty at the Council. Here is what he said in his introductory speech to the debates on November 19, 1963:[24]

- In defending religious freedom, we are not asserting that it is up to man to consider the religious problem as he sees fit, without the introduction of any moral obligation, and that he can decide as he pleases whether or not to embrace a religion (religious indifferentism).

- We do not claim that the human conscience is free in the sense that it is not subject to any law, i.e., that it is free from any obligation to God (secularism).

- We are not saying that one can consider the true and the false to have the same rights, as if there were no objective standard of truth (doctrinal relativism). . . .

If someone insisted on attributing to the expression "religious freedom" one of these meanings, he would be giving the text a meaning that is neither in its words nor in our intention. . . .

Religious freedom implies man's autonomy, not *ab intra*, but *ad extra*. *Ab intra*, man is not free from obligation in religious matters. *Ad extra*, his freedom is infringed when he cannot *obey the demands* of his conscience in religious matters.

Bishop De Smedt does not consider the case where man *disobeys* the demands of his conscience. He does not say,

---

[24] Bishop Emiel-Jozef De Smedt, "La Liberté religieuse: Continuité et progrès dans les enseignements du magistère," quoted in Bertrand de Margerie, *Liberté religieuse et Règne du Christ* (Paris: Cerf, 1988), 82–83.

but does not exclude, that *ad extra* man can sometimes be prevented from acting *against* his conscience. A door is left open to the clarification provided by Fr. Lucien.

a) A footnote in *DH* that refers to Leo XIII excludes relativism

In its definition of religious liberty, *DH* 2.1 refers in a footnote to a passage of the Encyclical *Libertas Præstantissimum*, no. 30, in which Leo XIII distinguishes two meanings of "religious liberty":

> Another liberty is widely advocated, namely, liberty of conscience. If by this is meant that everyone may, *as he chooses, worship God or not*, it is sufficiently refuted by the arguments already adduced. But it may also be taken to mean that *every man in the State may follow the will of God and, from a consciousness of duty and free from every obstacle, obey His commands*. This, indeed, is true liberty, a liberty worthy of the sons of God, which nobly maintains the dignity of man and is stronger than all violence or wrong—a liberty which the Church has always desired and held most dear. This is the kind of liberty the Apostles claimed for themselves with intrepid constancy, which the apologists of Christianity confirmed by their writings, and which the martyrs in vast numbers consecrated by their blood. And deservedly so; for this Christian liberty bears witness to the absolute and most just dominion of God over man, and to the chief and supreme duty of man toward God.[25]

---

[25] Leo XIII, Encyclical *Libertatis Præstantissimum* no. 30, *Acta Sanctæ Sedis* 20 (1887–88): 608, *DzH* 3250. English version available at papalencyclicals.net at https://www.papalencyclicals.net/leo13/l13liber.htm [accessed 08/07/2024].

Leo XIII's distinction contains the seeds of Fr. Lucien's thesis.

- To be able to worship or not worship God "as one chooses" is to *act as one wishes* in religious matters.

- The right to "follow the will of God and, from a consciousness of duty and free from every obstacle, obey His commands," corresponds to the right not to be prevented from *acting according to one's conscience* in religious matters.

Leo XIII says: "from a consciousness of duty." This seems to indicate that, even if man does not know the true will of God, he retains the right to act according to what he believes to be the divine will, i.e., according to his conscience. In any case, Leo XIII says that the expression "freedom of conscience" can have a Catholic meaning. So it is not doing violence to *DH* to read a Catholic meaning into it, especially since the conciliar text, precisely in its ambiguous passage, takes care to refer to a magisterial teaching which, by ruling out relativism, dispels this ambiguity.[26]

---

[26] Another indication that the Church has not given up her traditional doctrine is that the *Catechism of the Catholic Church*, no. 2109, teaches that the right to religious liberty must be limited "according to the requirements of the common good," and not only "by a 'public order'." *Catechism of the Catholic Church*, 2nd ed. (Washington, DC: United States Catholic Conference, Inc.—Libreria Editrice Vaticana, 1997), 512.

b) What is the Catholic attitude when the Magisterium expresses itself in an ambiguous manner?

This is learned at catechism, when we recite the *Act of Faith*:

> I believe these and all the truths which the holy Catholic Church teaches, because Thou hast revealed them, Who canst neither deceive nor be deceived.

Faith causes us to adhere to the Church's teaching. And this adherence of faith is global: it extends to all the truths taught by the Church through her magisterium.

This is why one cannot receive the teaching of the Magisterium when two magisterial texts contradict each other. It is in fact impossible to adhere to two formally contradictory propositions at the same time. By adhering to one, the faithful are forced to reject the other, and vice versa.

But if the two propositions *can* be reconciled, one returns *ipso facto* to the normal situation in which one receives the *entire* teaching of the magisterium. The same global adherence, which prevents one from receiving two contradictory teachings, demands that one interpret each teaching in coherence with all the others.[27] So, if one *can* interpret them in such a way as to remove the contradiction, one *must* do so. Fr. Lucien explains it well:

> Faced with a magisterial text—whether it is infallible or not, but truly "authentic"—every Catholic at first

---

[27] It would not be quite fair to dismiss Vatican II as incoherent with tradition, while refusing to understand the words of Vatican II in a sense that is coherent with tradition.

spontaneously (with the very spontaneity of the life of faith) adopts a habitual and global tendency towards adherence. To this attitude on the part of the faithful corresponds, on the side of any authentic magisterial statement, an essential aspect regarding its meaning: the most relevant *context* of an *authentic* magisterial text, precisely as *authentic*, is the totality of the revealed datum and, more precisely, the totality of what the Magisterium has already determined.

This is why, even in the case of a *simply* authentic text [i.e., not certainly infallible], the faithful's *a priori* attitude is one of *reception* and *comprehension* of its statements in a sense that conforms to the totality of former teaching.

Further, if a new text includes, in its actual wording, several possible interpretations (let's say two interpretations) of which one is *compatible* with former teaching and the other *contradictory* to it, it is the compatible interpretation that is the true meaning, the *magisterial and authentic* meaning, of the new document.[28]

It will be objected that many of the Council Fathers had "liberal" ideas, in the sense outlined above. Be that as it may, the private and subjective opinions of the Fathers cannot prevail over the objective and literal content of the promulgated text. Let us suppose that, at the time of the conciliar debates, some of the Fathers understood the expression "acting according to one's conscience" in a relativistic or liberal sense. Promulgation incorporates *DH* into the totality of magisterial texts. Once this text has been promulgated, the very same Fathers will have to receive it in coherence with all traditional teaching.

[28] Lucien, "Modest Follow-up," 28–29.

Pope Sixtus IV reiterated this rule of interpretation in his encyclical *Romani Pontificis Provida* of November 27, 1477:[29]

> Therefore, just as this Our holy and laudable desire may not be justly condemned by anyone, so also Our intention and sound mind, which aims only at an obvious good, must not be impugned by recourse to ambiguity, for it is *the rule in studying theology that any proposition containing a doubtful meaning should always be taken in that sense which renders the statement true.*

Fr. Lucien's interpretation, which leads to a true statement, is therefore to be preferred.

c) Did some of the Council Fathers share Fr. Lucien's interpretation?

An explanation of religious liberty similar to that of Fr. Lucien was presented to all the participants in the Conciliar Hall. During the 129th General Congregation, on September 16, 1965, Mgr. Luigi Carli, Bishop of Segni,[30] was the thirteenth Council Father to speak. He declared that he disagreed with the doctrine contained in the schema on religious liberty, which he summarized as follows (emphasis added):

> The truly new and, as it were, "neuralgic" thesis that underlies the whole schema, even though it is not

---

[29] Sixtus IV, Encyclical *Romani Pontificis Provida* (November 27, 1477), DzH 1407.

[30] Bishop Carli was a member of the conservative *Coetus internationalis Patrum.* According to Bernard Tissier de Mallerais, *Marcel Lefebvre. Une vie* (Paris: Clovis, 2002), 310, he was considered by many to be "the best theologian of the Council."

explicitly stated, is that *"man has a genuine* (i.e. real, not putative) *and objective* (i.e.: not merely subjective)—for it is asserted that it is based on the very dignity of the human person, that is, on the sum total of rights that the Author of Nature, God, has inalienably granted to every human being—*a natural right to be able, without any external impediment, to manifest externally and propagate his religious and moral ideas, however false or evil they may be, even among the followers of the one true religion, provided that he himself acts in good faith and within the limits established by the civil authority with regard to public order."*[31]

This interpretation of religious liberty is similar to Fr. Lucien's: the schema affirms the natural right to external freedom of action in religious matters, provided one is acting in good faith.[32] Bishop Carli criticizes this way of thinking, and argues that Christ in the Gospel, and St. Paul and St. John in their Letters, spoke severely against those who err and lead others into error. Thus, he says, the

---

[31] *Acta Synodalia*, IV, 1, 264: "Thesis vere nova et, ut ita dicam, nevralgica quae toti schemati, licet inexpressis verbis, subiacet eiusque veluti animam constituit, haec est: 'Homo habet verum (scil. reale minimeque putativum) et obiectivum (ergo: non tantummodo subiectivum) ius naturale—fundatum enim asseritur in ipsa dignitate personae humanae, i.e., in illa iurium summa quam Auctor naturae Deus omni homini inalienabiliter concessit—ius naturale ut sine ullo impedimento externo possit externe manifestare et propagare, etiam inter asseclas unius verae religionis, suas ideas religiosas et morales, licet obiective falsas aut malas, dummodo ipse sit in bona fide et agat intra limites ab auctoritate civili statutas intuitu ordinis publici.'"

[32] Bp. Carli uses the expression "in good faith," whereas *DH* would say "in accordance with his conscience." These two expressions largely overlap, but "in good faith" qualifies a person's habitual state, his subjective dispositions, which are difficult to judge from the outside, whereas "in accordance with his conscience" qualifies the morality of a specific act, which is often objectively observable.

above thesis does not provide a basis for the kind of total religious liberty that proponents of the schema advocate, "unless we say that Christ or Paul or John assumed that all the preachers of error in their day were of bad faith, just as, conversely, we assume that all of them in our day are of good faith!"[33]

We can see an interesting point in this somewhat hyperbolic conclusion. Bishop Carli saw that the religious liberty defined in the schema does *not apply* to the propagation of errors made "in bad faith." As he shows, this principle can lead the state to act in opposite ways, depending on whether it assumes that consciences are informed or not. If consciences are generally informed of the truth, the state will defend it more severely; if they are not, it will have to tolerate error. Bishop Carli realized that the Council's teaching on religious liberty could be interpreted in a way similar to what Fr. Lucien would propose many years later.

d) Since Vatican II, have the popes maintained the Church's traditional teaching on conscience?

1. They have reaffirmed that human intelligence is capable of objective knowledge.

Paul VI, Solemn Profession of Faith *Solemni Hac Liturgia* (June 30, 1968), no. 5:

> It is important in this respect to recall that, beyond scientifically verified phenomena, the intellect which God has given us reaches *that which is*, and not merely the

---

[33] *Acta Synodalia*, IV, 1, 265: "Nisi dicas sive Christum, sive Paulum, sive Ioannem falsos praedicatores sui temporis omnes in mala fide versari supposuisse, quemadmodum, e converso, nos nostri temporis omnes in bona fide versari supponimus!"

subjective expression of the structures and development of consciousness. . . .[34]

John Paul II, Encyclical *Veritatis Splendor* (August 6, 1993), no. 32. Here, the pope recalls St. Thomas's definition of conscience (emphasis added), which has been modified by modern subjectivism:

> Once the idea of a universal truth about the good, knowable by human reason, is lost, inevitably the notion of conscience also changes. Conscience is no longer considered in its primordial reality as *an act of a person's intelligence, the function of which is to apply the universal knowledge of the good in a specific situation and thus to express a judgment about the right conduct to be chosen here and now.* Instead, there is a tendency to grant to the individual conscience the prerogative of independently determining the criteria of good and evil and then acting accordingly. Such an outlook is quite congenial to an individualist ethic, wherein each individual is faced with his own truth, different from the truth of others.[35]

2. The post-conciliar magisterium condemned subjectivism and relativism

Vatican II, Pastoral Constitution *Gaudium et Spes* (December 7, 1965), no. 16:

---

[34] Paul VI, Solemn Profession of Faith *Solemni Hac Liturgia* (June 30, 1968), no. 5, *AAS* 60 (1968): 435. English version: *The Credo of the People of God Proclaimed by His Holiness, Pope Paul VI, June 30, 1968* (Boston, Mass.: Pauline Books & Media, 1996), 5.

[35] John Paul II, Encyclical *Veritatis Splendor* (August 6, 1993), no. 32, *AAS* 85 (1993): 1159–1160. English version: *The Splendor of Truth: Veritatis Splendor, Encyclical Letter, August 6, 1993* (Washington DC: United States Catholic Conference, 1993), 53.

Deep within their conscience individuals discover a law which they do not make for themselves but which they are bound to obey, whose voice, ever summoning them to love and do what is good and to avoid what is evil, rings in their heart when necessary with the command: Do this, keep away from that. For inscribed in their hearts by God, human beings have a law whose observance is their dignity and in accordance with which they are to be judged (Rom. 2:14–16). . . . And the more a correct conscience prevails, so much the more do persons and groups abandon blind whims and work to conform to the *objective norms of morality.*[36]

Paul VI, Encyclical *Ecclesiam Suam* (August 6, 1964), no. 28:

But the need for serious reflection on truths which are already well known is *in close accordance with the genius and mentality of our contemporaries,* who like to explore their minds in depth. They find mental repose in the secure grasp of truth, apprehended, as it were, in the light of conscience. Not that this method of enquiry is without *serious risk. Famous philosophers have studied this activity of the human intellect and pronounced it to be its most perfect and highest function. They have actually gone so far as to maintain that it is the measure and source of reality, and this has led them to some abstruse, barren, absurd, and wholly fallacious conclusions.* . . . [C]arefully coordinated with that habit of mind whereby a man discovers *objective truth,* the investigation of one's conscious knowledge may well lead to a greater

---

[36] Norman P. Tanner, SJ, ed., *Decrees of the Ecumenical Councils*, vol. 2, *Trent to Vatican II* (London: Sheed and Ward, and Washington DC: Georgetown University Press, 1990), 1077–78.

knowledge of oneself, one's dignity as a human being, one's intellectual powers and practical ability.[37]

John Paul II, *Veritatis Splendor*, no. 32:

Certain currents of modern thought have gone so far as to *exalt freedom to such an extent that it becomes an absolute, which would then be the source of values.* This is the direction taken by doctrines which have lost the sense of the transcendent or which are explicitly atheist. The individual conscience is accorded the status of a supreme tribunal of moral judgment which hands down categorical and infallible decisions about good and evil. *To the affirmation that one has a duty to follow one's conscience is unduly added the affirmation that one's moral judgment is true merely by the fact that it has its origin in the conscience.* But in this way the inescapable claims of truth disappear, yielding their place to a criterion of sincerity, authenticity and "being at peace with oneself," so much so that some have come to adopt a radically *subjectivistic* conception of moral judgment.[38]

Saint John Paul II had been a Council Father. According to the *Catechism of the Catholic Church* that he promulgated in 1992:

1792. Ignorance of Christ and his Gospel, bad example given by others, enslavement to one's passions, *assertion of a mistaken notion of autonomy of conscience*, rejection of the Church's authority and her teaching, lack of

---

[37] Paul VI, Encyclical *Ecclesiam Suam* (August 6, 1964), no. 28, *AAS* 56 (1964): 618–19. English version: Carlen, *Papal Encyclicals*, vol. 2, 140.

[38] John Paul II, Encyclical *Veritatis Splendor* (August 6, 1993), no. 32, *AAS* 85 (1993): 1159; English: *The Splendor of Truth*, 52–53.

conversion and of charity: these can be at the source of errors of judgment in moral conduct.[39]

Pope Benedict XVI was an expert at the time of the Council. In his address to the Roman Curia on December 20, 2010, he contrasts the modern conception of conscience with that of Newman:

> In modern thinking, the word "conscience" signifies that for moral and religious questions, it is the subjective dimension, the individual, that constitutes the final authority for decision. The world is divided into the realms of the objective and the subjective. To the objective realm belong things that can be calculated and verified by experiment. Religion and morals fall outside the scope of these methods and are therefore considered to lie within the subjective realm. Here, it is said, there are in the final analysis no objective criteria. The ultimate instance that can decide here is therefore the subject alone, and *precisely this is what the word "conscience" expresses: in this realm only the individual, with his intuitions and experiences, can decide.*

> Newman's understanding of conscience is diametrically opposed to this. *For him, "conscience" means man's capacity for truth: the capacity to recognize precisely in the decision-making areas of his life—religion and morals—a truth,* the *truth.* At the same time, conscience—man's capacity to recognize truth—thereby imposes on him the obligation to set out along the path towards truth, to seek it and to submit to it wherever he finds it. Conscience is both capacity for truth and obedience to the truth which manifests itself to anyone who seeks it

[39] CCC, 441.

with an open heart. The path of Newman's conversions is a path of conscience—not a path of self-asserting subjectivity but, on the contrary, a path of obedience to the truth that was gradually opening up to him.[40]

d) Answers to objections

First objection: how will the civil authority know whether an individual is acting according to his conscience, since it cannot read consciences?

My answer is that this is not necessary, because at least in some cases it is possible to observe, based on outside behavior, that someone is acting against his conscience. A large part of the work of the criminal courts consists in judging from the outside certain things that happen "inside" people. Let us read what a recent textbook for law students has to say.[41]

> *Intentional wrongdoing.* . . . In principle, felonies and misdemeanors are intentional offenses. . . . *Intention* is characterized by knowledge of the illegality of the facts, which does not include intent to harm. But even if an error regarding the law is a cause of non-responsibility (*Code pénal* 122–23), *no one is supposed to be ignorant of the law.*

To this knowledge must be added that of the factual reality: everything that contributes to the offence must

---

[40] Benedict XVI, Address on the Occasion of Christmas Greetings to the Roman Curia *È con vivo piacere* (December 20, 2010), *AAS* 103 (2011): 39–40. English version accessible at https://www.vatican.va/content/benedict-xvi/en/speeches/2010/december/documents/hf_ben-xvi_spe_20101220_curia-auguri.html [accessed 08/14/2024].

[41] Gérard Clément, Jean-Philippe Vincentini, Frédérique Dubost, *Fiches de droit pénal général*, 4th ed. (Paris: Éditions Ellipses, 2013), 87–90.

be known. For example, article 227–8 of the *Code pénal*, which punishes the abduction of a minor child without fraud or violence, requires knowledge of the child's minority. Intention is also characterized by the will to accomplish the material element of the offence as described by the qualifying text, coupled with the will to achieve the outcome that was reached or could have been reached.

The criminal law judge examines whether the accused has knowledge of the law and the facts (does he know that these concrete facts are a transgression of the law?), whether he has the will to commit the facts. . . . All this without penetrating the conscience or accessing the internal forum of the accused.

> Because of the presumption of innocence, it is up to the prosecution to prove intent. *In most cases, intent can be inferred from the very nature of the material conduct, if it is unequivocal.* . . . Intention can also be inferred from a simple presumption of guilt. In the case of possession of stolen goods, knowledge of the fraudulent origin of the thing possessed can be established on the basis of a number of clues, such as: the conditions of purchase; the price; the place of sale; the respective professions of seller and buyer. On the other hand, in the case of offences where the material element is equivocal, proof of intent is established by a presumption of fact. Thus, intent to cause death to another person may be deemed to have been established on the basis of a number of clues, such as: the weapon used; firing direction; body part aimed at and hit; number of shots. . . .

The courts are therefore able, to a certain extent, to judge whether an exterior act has been committed with knowledge and will. They do this *indirectly* by carefully examining the behavior of the defendant. In the example above, the defendant is presumed to be aware of the law prohibiting the possession of stolen goods. It is established from his behavior that he knows the fact of the fraudulent origin of the thing. Therefore, in applying the law to this particular case, his conscience necessarily told him not to possess the stolen item. However, his behavior shows that he voluntarily possessed it. Therefore, he acted against his conscience.

It will be objected that, in so doing, civil authority judges only the external act, not the internal forum, of which God alone is the judge. The reply is that when human authority judges a man's external act, it judges it *as a human act*, voluntary and free, i.e. made under the power of the will directed by reason. Now, there is no human act without a judgment of conscience, and no fault without an act against one's conscience. Thus, even if the authority judges only the external act, reserving the ultimate judgment of the internal forum to God, it nonetheless pronounces on the fact that, *as far as can be judged from the external act*, the person has acted against his conscience.

In this respect it is worth quoting the *Code of Canon Law* c. 1321.3:

> When an external violation has occurred, imputability is presumed unless it is otherwise apparent.[42]

If it is indeed this person who committed the act, and if the act, as it appears externally, is a voluntary violation of the law, one *presumes* that his person has voluntarily

---

[42] *Code of Canon Law. Latin-English Edition. New English Translation Prepared under the Auspices of the Canon Law Society of America* (Washington, DC: Canon Law Society of America—Libreria Editrice Vaticana, 1989), 412.

violated the law. One cannot voluntarily violate a norm recognized as obligatory, however, without acting against one's conscience. This explains why, at certain times, the civil authorities were able to find certain people guilty of having acted against their conscience in religious matters.

Second objection: *DH* asserts that religious liberty exists in those who do not live up to their obligation of seeking the truth; does this not contradict Fr Lucien's interpretation of *DH*?

DH no. 2.2 asserts:

> [T]he right to this immunity continues to exist even in those who do not live up to their obligation of seeking the truth and adhering to it and the exercise of this right is not to be impeded, provided that just public order be observed.

This objection would be valid if, in order to enjoy religious liberty, one had to have an upright conscience, i.e., have done one's utmost to know the truth. However, the Council does not base religious liberty on uprightness of conscience. Said liberty exists regardless of whether or not one has made the effort to seek the truth. It is not the earnestness of one's research or the quality of one's conscience that grants the right to religious liberty; one's action is protected by religious liberty through the simple fact that *it is an act according to one's conscience.*

But this in no way invalidates Fr. Lucien's thesis. Indeed, since man is capable of reaching the truth objectively placed at his disposal, there are truths (norms or facts) that cannot be ignored, and which each person includes in his or her judgment of conscience, either because these truths are universally recognized, such as the prohibition of murder or theft, or because these truths are well known in a given place and time. Such, for example, are the immorality in the twenty-first-century West of racism or the fact of the genocide of the Jews; in thirteenth-century Europe, such were the immorality of adultery and the fact of Christ's resurrection.

When, in the contemporary West, the State prosecutes racist acts, it does not ask whether those who commit them have "fulfilled the obligation to investigate" whether racism is illicit; rather it considers that all citizens know that racism is illicit and contrary to societal values. They need not seek out this truth. Similarly, in religious matters, anyone who acts against a well-known truth cannot claim to be following his conscience. He cannot therefore benefit from religious liberty for this act.

Third objection: does not accepting religious liberty amount to condemning certain historical practices of the Church (the evangelization of the Americas, the Inquisition, etc.)?

a) The repression of heresy by Christian rulers
At certain times in history, Christian rulers prosecuted heresy as such. In these cases, they did not act primarily as a civil power, but as the "secular arm" of the Church. The Church has always taught[43] that it has a certain right to impose penalties on clerics and laymen alike.[44] For certain penalties, She appeals to the civil power, which is thus subordinate to the Church. It is not the civil power that

---

[43] Thus the *Code of Canon Law* (1983), c. 1364.1, stipulates that "[a]n apostate from the faith, a heretic or a schismatic incurs a *latæ sententiæ* excommunication."

[44] The Declaration *DH* implicitly recognizes these rights of the Church when it asserts that "religious liberty . . . leaves whole and entire the traditional Catholic teaching concerning the moral duty, owed by men and by societies, towards the true religion and the sole Church of Christ." (*DH* no. 1).

decides, it simply puts itself at the disposal of the spiritual power. Of course, this elevation of the State's own power can only occur in societies that have received revelation, where "Christian values [are] integrated in the structure of society," as Cardinal Journet explains with regard to medieval Christianity.[45]

The Inquisition, at least in its legitimate mode of operation, did not condemn *material heretics*, i.e. those who unwittingly or unknowingly professed errors against the faith. After a trial, it would condemn a *formal heretic*, especially if he was convicted of pertinacity, i.e., persisted in error after having been proven wrong (which implies acting against his conscience). Thus, the Inquisition took into consideration both objective error *and also* the subjective imputability of persons.

b) The era of the great missions to South America
The Church has always called for "inviting" those "outside the bosom of the Church" to the faith, peacefully, through "preaching and example."[46] Contrary to a certain "black legend," the evangelization of the peoples of Central and South America was not the result of coercion; it was achieved especially through the efforts of the many missionaries sent among native peoples.

The First Provincial Council of America, meeting in 1552 in Lima, Peru, specifically stipulated:[47]

---

[45] Charles Journet, *The Church of the Word Incarnate: An Essay in Speculative Theology*, vol. 1, *The Apostolic Hierarchy*, trans. A.H.C. Downes (London: Sheed and Ward, 1955), 222.

[46] Paul III, Brief *Pastorale Officium* to the archbishop of Toledo (May 29, 1537), *DzH* 1495.

[47] Ruben Ugarte Varga, SJ, *Concilios Limenses (1551–1772)* (Lima: Tipografía peruana, 1951), 1.11. *Constitución 7ª* — *Que ninguno sea baptizado contra su voluntad*. Otrosí, por cuanto, conforme a la doctrina de nuestro maestro y redentor Jesucristo, ninguno ha de ser compelido a recibir nuestra santa fe católica, sino persuadido y atraído

Constitution 7—Let none be baptized against his will.
Further, since, according to the teaching of our Master
and Redeemer Jesus Christ, no one must be compelled
to receive our holy Catholic Faith, unless persuaded and
attracted by its truth and liberty, as well as by the reward
of blessedness . . ., let no one baptize any Indian aged
eight years and older without having first learned from
him whether he is coming of his will and out of love for
what he is seeking and receives, and that he understands
it, just as has been said, and let no one baptize the child
of any infidel before the age of reason against the will
of his parents or guardians.

Furthermore, it is only in villages peopled by Christians
that this council calls for the destruction of pagan temples
and idols. The Church does not reckon herself authorized
to demand that the Spanish civil authorities proceed to
such a destruction *in villages of infidels*; the council merely
invites churchmen to "consult" the authorities to obtain
this sort of measure from them [48].

Although we may find these measures frankly excessive
(if not unjust), they do not contradict in principle the
religious liberty defined by *DH*, in the sense defended by
Fr. Lucien. To legitimize the destruction of pagan oratories, the Council of Lima did not base itself solely on the
objective falsehood of pagan religions. It invoked the fact
that these idolatrous oratories are "contrary to the natural
law" accessible to every human being; that they constitute

con la verdad y libertad della, y con el premio de la bienaventuranza
[...] que ninguno baptice a indio ocho años arriba, sin que primero
entienda dél si viene de su voluntad, y por amor que tenga a lo que
pide y recibe, y lo entienda, según y como dicho es ni baptice ningún
niño de infiel antes que llegue a uso de razón, contra la voluntad de
sus padres o de las personas que los tienen a cargo.

[48] *Ibid.*, 8–9.

a temptation for indigenous Christians to fall into the sin of idolatry (an act that would be contrary to their conscience); finally, these oratories could prevent certain pagans from becoming Christians (if there were a sin of infidelity, it would be an act contrary to their conscience).

c) Secular societies

In our de-Christianized societies, we cannot assume that the truths of faith are commonplace. Even predominantly Catholic societies find themselves steeped in scientistic and relativistic prejudices that strip Christian truths of their commonplace and undisputed character. Violators of that religion are no longer presumed to be acting against their conscience. This is why, even in "Catholic countries," the State does not prosecute them, and does not put its secular arm at the service of the Church as it did in other eras.

Conversely, as we have seen, Catholics normally follow their conscience in practicing their faith. Against the oppression of atheistic or Islamic states, they have the right to act according to their conscience. This is what Leo XIII teaches in *Libertas Præstantissimum*: "But it may also be taken to mean that every man in the State may follow the will of God and, from a consciousness of duty and free from every obstacle, obey His commands."[49] This is a response to the concern expressed by Bishop De Smedt when he explained to the Council Fathers why the Church should proclaim religious liberty:

> Many non-Catholics feel some aversion towards the Church, or at least suspect it of a certain Machiavellianism. It seems to them that we demand the free exercise of religion when Catholics are few in number in a country

---

[49] Leo XIII, Encyclical *Libertas Præstantissimum* (June 20, 1888), no. 30, *DzH* 3250.

but despise and deny this same religious liberty when Catholics are in the majority. [50]

Contrary to what is sometimes seen in Islam, the Church does not change her principles. The corollary of freedom to act according to one's conscience is that religious acts cannot be prevented unless they are committed culpably (against one's conscience). So if the Church demands freedom for minority Catholics and non-Catholics alike, it is not because Catholics cannot assert themselves when they are in the minority, but in the name of *justice*. Catholics practice their religion according to their conscience; outside of a fully Catholic society, it cannot be assumed that the practices of infidels or heretics are culpable or committed against their conscience. And if, in Christendom, the State sometimes prevents acts contrary to Catholicism, it is not because the Church is in a position of strength; it is because in Christendom the State rightly presumes that violators of the Catholic religion are guilty of acting against their conscience.

CONCLUSION

The strength of Fr. Lucien's solution lies in its explanatory power. It is not a question of "saving Vatican II at any cost," including the cost of all plausibility. Our author's thesis not only avoids contradiction, but also explains the appearance of contradiction. Modern relativism distorts the traditional conception of conscience and thus produces the ambiguity we denounced in the text of *DH*.

- This explains why the expression "freedom of conscience" can refer to a doctrine condemned

[50] Bishop Emiel-Jozef De Smedt, "La Liberté religieuse," 81–82.

by the Church ("everyone is free to think what he wishes, and therefore to act as he wishes").

- This explains why *DH*'s definition of religious liberty, ("the right to act according to one's conscience"), bears a striking resemblance to the false doctrine condemned by the Church.

- Conversely, this explains how religious liberty as defined by *DH* can have an entirely true and traditional meaning.

Perhaps this explains the link established by the Council between the right to religious liberty and human dignity. It is part of man's dignity to follow the duty his conscience dictates. Those who follow their conscience are more worthy than those who do not. Indeed, one cannot disobey one's conscience without sin, and sin is contrary to human dignity.

All that remained was to show that the Council does indeed use the expression "to act according to one's conscience" in the traditional realist sense. The proof lies in the Council itself. *DH* refers to a text by Leo XIII that rejects relativism and seems to suggest Fr. Lucien's thesis in advance. And then there is the general argument: when the magisterium expresses itself ambiguously, a possible interpretation that leads to a true affirmation *must* be preferred.

This thesis has another argument in its favor. It removes the contradiction by means of the traditional doctrine on conscience, a doctrine which has the merit of having been reaffirmed by the popes since Vatican II. The continuity of these Popes' teaching on moral conscience confirms the "hermeneutic of continuity" applied by Fr. Lucien to *DH*.

A final argument, that of fittingness, may be invoked. Religious liberty as defined by Vatican II not only does not contradict the Church's earlier doctrine: it deepens it. Nineteenth-century popes speak of liberty from the point of view of the civil authority that governs society by implementing a more or less broad religious toleration. *DH* speaks of liberty from the point of view of the individual. Only if it is known can truth impose duties on the conscience. When he knows the truth, when it informs his conscience, the individual has no right to act against it.

In this way, *DH* offers a unifying principle between the doctrine of tolerance and that of the liberty of the Church. In the name of the rights of *known* truth, religious liberty protects both those who are in error through no (certain) fault of their own, and also true religion, whether against a persecuting State, or against its violators in an entirely Catholic society. This ability to unify diverse elements argues in favor of the solution proposed by Fr. Lucien.

APPENDIX

Dignitatis Humanæ Declaration on Religious Liberty

Translated by Michael Pakaluk, Ph.D.

1.

Men in this age are becoming daily more aware of the dignity of the human person. The number of those is growing who insist that men, in their actions, should enjoy and make use of their own counsel and responsible liberty, not forced by coercive means, but led in conscience by the recognition of a duty.

Moreover, they demand that limits in law be placed on public authorities, so that the virtuous liberty of persons and of associations is not excessively restricted.

This insistence on liberty in human society especially concerns goods of the human spirit, most fundamentally, those which pertain to the free exercise in society of religion.

This Vatican Council, taking careful note of these aspirations of the human spirit, and proposing to declare the extent to which these aspirations are in conformity with truth and justice, searches diligently the sacred tradition and doctrine of the Church, from which it brings forth new things which are, without exception, in harmony with the old.

Accordingly, this Sacred Council professes first of all that God Himself has made known to the human race a pathway by which, through serving Him, men can be made whole and completely happy in Christ. This single, true Religion, we believe, subsists in the Catholic and apostolic Church, to which the Lord Jesus entrusted the responsibility of spreading this Religion to all men without exception, when he told the Apostles, "Go, therefore, and make disciples of all nations, baptizing them in the name of the Father, and of the Son, and of the holy Spirit, teaching them to observe all that I have commanded you," (Mt. 28:19–20). Indeed all men are bound, especially in matters which concern God and His Church, to seek the truth; to embrace it, when known by them; and to safeguard it.

This Sacred Council similarly professes that these obligations reach through to and bind the consciences of men. Nor is there any other way for truth to impose itself except by the force of truth itself, which penetrates sweetly and yet at the same time strongly into the human mind.

On the other hand, religious liberty involves an immunity from coercion in civil society, which men insist upon in carrying out their duty of giving honor to God. Religious liberty therefore leaves whole and entire the traditional Catholic teaching concerning the moral duty, owed by men and by societies, towards the true religion and the sole Church of Christ. But beyond that, this Sacred Council, in taking up the matter of religious liberty, intends to expound the teaching of recent Popes concerning the inviolable rights of the human person and the juridical structure of society.

I. THE NATURE OF RELIGIOUS LIBERTY IN GENERAL

2.

This Vatican Council declares that a human person has a right to religious liberty. This type of liberty consists in the fact that, within necessary limits, all men need to be immune from coercion, whether deriving from individuals, social groups, or any human authority, in any matter of religion, in such a way that no one is either forced to act against his conscience, or impeded from acting in accordance with his conscience, regardless of whether he is acting in private or in public, alone or in association with others.

Moreover it declares that the right to religious liberty is, in truth, based on the very dignity of the human person, which is known both through the revealed Word of God and by reason itself. This right of the human person to religious liberty should be recognized in the juridical structure of a society in such a way that it finds expression as a civil right.

All men without exception, on account of their dignity, because they are persons, that is to say, beings endowed with reason and freewill, and adorned with the gift of personal responsibility, are not only impelled by their own nature, but also bound by a moral obligation, to seek that truth which religion most fundamentally is concerned with. They are moreover bound to embrace the truth once it is known, and to order their entire life according to the requirements of the truth. Men cannot satisfy this obligation, in a manner which befits their distinctive nature, unless they enjoy psychological liberty together with an immunity from external coercion. The right to religious liberty, therefore, is not based on any subjective disposition of a person, but rather in the very nature of a person. That is why the right to this immunity remains even in those who do not meet their obligation to seek the truth and embrace it, and why the exercise of this right cannot be impeded (assuming that, in that exercise, a just public order is maintained).

3.

These conclusions appear in an even clearer light if one considers that the highest authority for human life is the divine law itself—eternal, objective, and universal—by which God, deliberating in his wisdom and love, orders, directs, and governs the whole world and the paths taken by the human community. God gives man the opportunity to be a sharer in this law of God, so that, as divine providence "orders things sweetly," man becomes gives increasing recognition to unchangeable divine truth. That is why each person has a duty, and therefore also a right, of seeking the truth in matters of religion—in order that each person, through those means truly suited to him, might wisely form his own correct and true judgments of conscience.

Again, truth when sought after needs to be pursued in the manner which matches the dignity of the human person and his social nature, that is, through an inquiry which is liberal, aided by a teaching authority or course of instruction, and with the assistance of communication and dialogue, through which men propose to one another the truth they have found or believe to have found, so that they can help one another in the search for truth; again, truth once known needs to be adhered to firmly through a personal assent.

Indeed, man perceives and discerns the indications of the divine law through the medium of his own conscience, which he is obliged to follow faithfully in all of his actions, so that he might find his way to God, his final goal. Therefore, he must not be forced to act contrary to his conscience. But neither should he be hindered from acting in accordance with his conscience, especially in matters of religion. For the exercise of religion, of its very nature, consists most fundamentally in interior and free acts of the will, by which a man orders himself directly to God. Acts like that cannot be commanded or prohibited by any merely human authority. Yet the social nature of man requires that man give external expression to his interior acts of religion: since, when he communicates with others in some matter of religion, he professes his own religion in a communitarian manner. Therefore, an injury is done to the human person, and to the order established by God for men, if man is denied the free exercise of religion in society (assuming that, in that exercise, a just public order is maintained).

Besides, religious acts, by which men whether privately or publicly, out of the convictions of their hearts, order themselves to God, by their nature transcend the earthly and temporal order of things. Therefore, civil authority, the specific end of which is care of the temporal common good, needs actually to recognize the religious life of citizens and encourage it. But civil authority must be said to be overstepping its specific limits, if it should presume to direct or impede religious acts.

4.

The liberty, or immunity from coercion, in matters of religion, which pertains to persons considered individually, must be acknowledged to pertain also to persons acting in concert. After all, that there should be communities of a religious character is implied both by the social nature of man and by religion itself.

These communities, therefore, need an immunity under the law (assuming that, in their enjoyment of this immunity, the requirements of a just public order are not violated), so that they can conduct themselves in accordance with their own distinctive norms, render honor to the Supreme Divinity in public worship, aid their members in the practice of religious life and strengthen them with instruction, and promote those institutions, in which their members work together to follow their own distinctive way of life in accordance with their religious principles.

Similarly religious communities have a right not to be hindered, either by legal measures or by the administrative actions of civil authorities, in selecting, educating, appointing, and transferring their own ministers, in communications with religious authorities or with communities at work in other parts of the world, in the construction of religious buildings, and, not least, in acquiring and enjoying appropriate goods.

Religious communities also have a right not to be hindered in teaching and bearing witness to their faith in public, whether in speech or in writing. However, in spreading religious faith, and in introducing religious practices, one should always abstain from every kind of action which smacks of coercion, or illicit persuasion, or persuasion which is less than upright, especially when one is dealing with the uneducated or persons in need. That sort of action should be regarded as an abuse of one's own right and as an attack on the rights of others.

Religious liberty additionally comes into play, in insuring that religious communities are not prohibited from freely demonstrating the special power of their teaching for the good ordering of society and for bringing life to human activity in its entirety.

Finally, the social nature of man, and the nature of religion itself, are the foundation for the right by which men, moved by their own particular religious sense, are able freely to hold meetings and to form educational, cultural, charitable and social associations.

5.

Each family has the right freely to order its own domestic religious life under the guidance of the parents. It does so as a society which enjoys its own distinctive and primordial right. The parents in particular have a right to determine, in accordance with their own religious convictions, the nature of the religious instruction passed on to their children. Moreover, civil authorities must recognize the right of parents to select, with genuine liberty, schools or other means of education, nor should any unjust burdens be placed, directly or indirectly, upon this liberty of selection. Additionally, the rights of the parents are violated if their children are forced to attend classes which are at odds with the religious convictions of their parents, or if a single type of education is imposed, which entirely excludes religious formation.

6.

Since the common good of society, which is the sum total of those conditions of social life, by which men are able to pursue their perfection more fully and more expeditiously, consists above all in the rights and duties distinctive of the human person, the care of the right to religious liberty falls in part upon citizens, in part upon social groups, in part upon civil authorities, and in part upon the Church and other religious communities, in the manner appropriate for each, depending upon the responsibility which each of these has for the common good.

To superintend and promote the inviolable rights of man is essentially bound up with the duties of any civil authority whatsoever. It follows that each civil authority is bound, through just laws and through other appropriate measures, to undertake the effective superintendence of the religious liberty of all of its citizens, and to supply in abundance those conditions which foster a religious way of life, with the aim that its citizens might be well positioned to exercise the right and fulfill the responsibilities of religion, so that society might enjoy the goods of justice and peace, which originate in the faithfulness of men towards God and towards His holy will.

If, in response to the particular circumstances of a people, special civil recognition is accorded, in the legal structure of the body politic, to one religious community, it is necessary that, at the same time, the right to liberty in matters of religion, of all citizens and all religious communities, be recognized and observed.

Finally, civil authority needs to insure that the equality of citizens before the law, which is a component of the common good of society, is never violated, either openly or in secret, because of considerations of religion, nor that there be any discrimination among citizens.

Whence it follows that a public authority commits an execrable crime, if by force, by fear, or by any other means, it imposes upon the citizens the profession or rejection of any religion, or if it impedes the citizens from joining or leaving any religious community. And how much more does it go against the will of God and against the sacred rights of the person and of the family of nations, when force is applied with the aim of destroying or suppressing religion simply!—whether this be throughout the human race in its entirety, or in some geographical region, or within some particular group.

7.

Human society is the context in which the right to liberty in matters of religion is exercised. Hence, the use of this liberty is subject to identifiable governing norms.

In the use of any liberty, the moral principle of personal and social responsibility needs to be observed: individual men and social groups, when exercising the rights that belong to them, are obliged by the moral law, to take into account the rights of others, their own duties toward others, and the common good of all—since we must act in accordance with justice and humanity in our dealings with everyone.

Again, since civil society has the right to protect itself against those abuses which can take place under the pretext of religious liberty, the task of providing that sort of protection pertains especially to civil authorities. Nevertheless this should not be carried out in an arbitrary way, or in such a way as to favor one party over another, but rather in accordance with those legal norms, conformable to the objective moral order, which are required (1) for the effective safeguarding of, and the peaceful settlement of conflicts among, the rights of all citizens, (2) for the adequate care of that honorable public peace which amounts to ordered life in common in true justice, and (3) for the required protection of public morality. All of these together form a basic part of the common good and fall under the definition of "public order."

Assuming these things are in place, then the customary principle of the fullness of liberty in society should be upheld, according to which liberty should be recognized by men to the fullest extent possible and should not be restricted, except on the occasion when, and to the extent that, it is necessary to do so.

8.

In our age for a variety of reasons men are subject to pressures and face the danger that they become shorn of the free decision-making that belongs to them. Yet also, on the other hand, there are not a few men who seem set on rejecting, under the appearance of liberty, any form of subordination, and who treat rightful obedience as a small matter.

For this reason, this Vatican Council exhorts everyone, especially those who have responsibility for the education of others, to take trouble to form men, who, precisely because they place themselves under a moral order, obey legitimate authority, and who are true lovers of liberty: men, to be sure, who by the decision-making that belongs to them, will determine a matter in the light of truth; who will carry out their activities with a sense of responsibility; and who will endeavor to promote whatever is true and just, gladly cooperating with others in their own tasks.

Religious liberty therefore needs to be in the service of, and should be ordered to, this goal as well: namely, that men in the fulfillment of their own responsibilities comport themselves with greater responsibility in social life.

II. Liberty by the light of Revelation

9.

These matters, which this Vatican Council declares about the right of man to religious liberty, have their foundation in the dignity of the person, the requirements of which have become more amply recognized by human reason from centuries of experience. Yet at the same time, this teaching about liberty has roots in divine Revelation—all the more reason, then, why Christians should keenly defend it.

Now, although Revelation does not explicitly affirm the right to immunity from external coercion in religious matters, still, (i) it makes evident the dignity of the human person in its complete fullness, (ii) it draws attention to the respect which Christ showed toward the liberty of man, in man's correspondence to the duty of believing the word of God, and (iii) it instructs us as regards the Spirit, which disciples of such a Master should recognize and follow in everything. In all these ways Revelation illuminates the general principles on which the doctrine of this Declaration of Religious Liberty is founded, in particular, that religious liberty is the perfect counterpart, in the context of human society, to the liberty of the act of Christian faith.

10.

The very foremost among these principles of Catholic doctrine, contained in the word of God, and constantly preached by the Fathers, is that man, in the act of believing, must respond to God of his own accord. Therefore, no one who is reluctant should be forced into embracing the faith. The reason is that the act of faith, of its very nature, is a free act—since man, who is redeemed by Christ the Savior, and called into the adoption of sons through Jesus Christ, is not able to cling to God as He reveals Himself, except the Father should draw him, and he, reasonably and freely, should surrender himself in obedience to God in faith. Therefore, it is entirely consonant with the inherent nature of faith that, in matters of religion, any type of external force on the part of men be excluded. The logic of religious liberty, then, makes no small contribution to encouraging that condition of things in which men are able easily to be invited to share in the Christian faith, to embrace it spontaneously, and to profess it eagerly in their entire way of life.

11.

Indeed, God calls men to His service in spirit and in truth, and, as a result, men are bound in conscience—and yet they are not coerced. The reason is that God has regard for the dignity of the human person created by Him, which needs to be guided by his own counsel and needs to enjoy liberty. This regard is most apparent in Christ Jesus, in whom God made Himself and His ways perfectly clear. For Christ, who is our Master and Lord, and at the same time meek and humble of heart, attracted and invited disciples with patience. When he used miracles to highlight and confirm his teaching, he did so in order to enliven and confirm the faith of those who listened to his preaching, not to achieve some kind of coercive effect in them.

To be sure, he decried lack of belief in his listeners. But he left vengeance to God on the Day of Judgment. When he sent the Apostles into the world, he said to them, "He who believes and is baptized will be saved, and he who does not believe will be condemned" (Mk 16:16). But knowing full well that weeds had been sown amidst the wheat, he gave the order that both should be left to grow until the harvest which is to take place at the end of time. Not wanting to be a political Messiah or someone who rules by force, he preferred to call himself the "Son of Man" who has come "to serve and to give his own life as a ransom for many" (Mk. 10:45). He showed Himself the perfect Servant of God, who "does not break the bruised reed nor extinguish the smoking flax" (Matt. 12:20). He recognized civil authority and its rights, commanding that tribute be given to Caesar. However, he gave clear warning that the higher rights of God are to be kept inviolate: "Render to Caesar the things that are Caesar's and to God the things that are God's" (Matt. 22:21). In the end, when he fulfilled the work of our redemption on the cross, by which he won for us men salvation and true freedom, He brought His own revelation to perfect completion: for He bore witness to the truth, while yet he declined to impose the truth by force on those who contradicted it. The reason is that his kingship is not enforced by violence from without. Rather, it is established by one's testifying to the truth, and by the hearing of the truth, and it grows by the love by which Christ as exalted upon the cross draws all men to Himself.

The Apostles, instructed by both the word and the example of Christ, took the same approach. From the first beginnings of the Church, these followers of Christ labored strenuously with the aim that all men be converted to confess Christ as Lord, yet not by coercive action nor by measures unworthy of the Gospel, but most fundamentally by the power of the word of God. With courage they proclaimed to one and all the plan of God our Savior, "who wills that all men should be saved and come to the acknowledgment of the truth" (1 Tim. 2:4). However, they showed respect for those who were weak, even if they continued in error, demonstrating in this way in what way "each one of us is to render to God an account of himself" (Romans 14:12) and the degree to which each of us is obliged to obey his own conscience. Like Christ, the Apostles were always intent on bearing witness to the truth of God, daring with an abundance of audacity before the people and before princes to speak "the word of God with confidence" (Acts 4:31). With a firm faith they held the Gospel truly to be of itself the power of God for salvation to everyone who has faith. Therefore, casting aside "carnal weapons," and following the gentle and unassuming example set by Christ, they preached the word of God with complete confidence in the power of this divine word to destroy all authorities opposed to God and to bring all men to the faith and obedience of Christ. The Apostles recognized legitimate civil authority, just as their Master did: "For there is no power except from God," the Apostle teaches, and thereafter commands: "Let everyone be subject to higher authorities.... He who resists authority resists God's ordinance" (Romans 13:1–5). At the same time, however, they were not afraid to contradict public authority when it set itself in opposition to the holy will of God: "It is necessary to obey God rather than men" (Acts 5:29). This is the approach which has been taken by innumerable martyrs and other faithful throughout the ages and across the whole earth.

12.

Therefore, the Church, faithful to the truth of the Gospel, follows the approach of Christ and the Apostles, when it recognizes and promotes the logic of religious liberty as in harmony with the dignity of man and the revelation of God. The Church has kept safe and handed down throughout the ages the teaching it received from the Master and from the Apostles. Even if, from the vicissitudes of the pilgrimage of human history, there has sometimes existed, in the life of the People of God, a manner of acting that was less in conformity with the spirit of the Gospel, or even opposed to it, nevertheless the doctrine of the Church that no one is to be forced into the faith has always stood firm.

Thus the leaven of the Gospel has long been operative in the minds of men and has worked a significant effect, such that men in the course of time have recognized more widely the dignity which is distinctive of their own person, and the conviction has attained full maturity that, in political society, in matters of religion, an immunity from any kind of human coercion should be upheld.

13.

Among the things that concern the good of the Church, and indeed the good of the earthly city, and which need to be always and everywhere upheld and defended against every injury, this certainly is preeminent, namely, that the Church should enjoy that degree of liberty which her care for the salvation of men requires. The reason is that this liberty is a sacred liberty, with which the Only-Begotten Son endowed the Church, after purchasing this liberty with His own blood. This liberty is so very distinctive an attribute of the Church, that anyone who impugns it, acts against the will of God. The liberty of the Church is the fundamental principle relevant to the relations between the Church and public authorities, and the whole civil order.

In human society, and in the face of any public authority, the Church claims by right a liberty for itself, as a spiritual authority, established by Christ, to which, by divine mandate, there falls the responsibility of going into the whole world and proclaiming the Gospel to every creature. The Church likewise claims by right a liberty for herself, insofar as it is additionally an association of men, who each and together enjoy the right to live in civil society in accordance with the precepts of the Christian faith.

It must be admitted that, when the logic of religious liberty goes beyond mere proclamation in words, or mere endorsement law, but in addition is applied in practice with sincerity, then the Church attains a certain stability, and a position of right and of fact, sufficient for the independence it needs to fulfil its divine mission. This independence in society is what church authorities have with greater and greater emphasis demanded by right. At the same time, too, in such a case, the Christian faithful enjoy the same civil right as other men not to be hindered in living their life in accordance with their conscience. Therefore, one finds a harmonious agreement between the liberty of the Church, and that religious liberty, pertaining to individual men without exception, and to communities, which requires recognition and endorsement as a right in the legal order.

14.

The Catholic Church, to correspond to the divine command, "teach all nations" (Mt. 28:19–20), needs to work strenuously with urgent concern, "that the word of God be spread abroad and glorified" (2 Thess. 3:1).

Mindful of this, the Church implores its own children, first of all, that "supplications, prayers, petitions, acts of thanksgiving be made for all men.... For this is good and agreeable in the sight of God our Savior, who wills that all men be saved and come to the knowledge of the truth" (1 Tim. 2:1–4).

Moreover, the Christian faithful in forming their consciences must pay careful attention to the holy and certain doctrine of the Church. For by the will of Christ the Church is the teacher of the truth, and its office is to articulate and authentically teach that truth which is Christ Himself; and, at the same time, by its own authority, it declares and confirms the basic principles of the moral order, which flow from human nature itself. Furthermore, may Christians, walking in wisdom to meet those who are without, "in the Holy Spirit, in unaffected love, in the word of truth" (2 Cor. 6:6–7), be about their task of spreading the light of life with all confidence and apostolic courage, even to the shedding of their blood.

Assuredly, each disciple is bound by a grave obligation toward Christ, his Master, each day to come to know more fully the truth received from Him, to proclaim it faithfully, and to defend it strenuously—on the assumption that means that are contrary to the spirit of the gospel are excluded. At the same time, nonetheless, the charity of Christ urges him to deal with love, patience, and good judgment, with men who continue in error or ignorance as concerns the faith. What he must take into account are (i) his duties toward Christ the life-giving Word, which is to be proclaimed; (ii) the rights of the human person; and (iii) the measure of grace given by God through Christ to man, who is invited to accept and profess the faith of their own accord.

15.

It holds true that men of the present time hope to be able freely to profess their religion whether in private or in public, and indeed religious liberty is now declared to be a civil right in most constitutions, and it is solemnly recognized in international documents.

And yet there is no lack of regimes in which, even if the liberty of religious worship is recognized in their constitution, nevertheless public authorities themselves strive to keep citizens from professing any religion, and they make life difficult and even dangerous for religious communities.

Greeting the first with joy as an auspicious sign of our times, while denouncing the other with sorrow as something to be deplored, this Sacred Council exhorts Catholics, and it implores men in general, to consider with utmost care how necessary religious liberty is, especially in the present condition of the human family. For it is obvious that all nations are day by day becoming more of a unity. Men diverse in culture and religion are joined together on closer grounds, and they are growing in their awareness of the personal responsibility of each. Accordingly, in order that peaceful relationships and harmonious agreement be established and strengthened, there is a need that religious liberty be everywhere protected with an effective legal safeguard, and that the highest duty and right, namely, of leading a religious life freely in society, be observed.

May the God and Father of all grant that the human family through diligently safeguarding the logic of religious liberty in society be brought by the grace of Christ and the power of the Holy Spirit to the sublime and everlasting "liberty in glory of the sons of God" (Rom 8:21).

ABOUT THE AUTHORS

Born in 1952, Fr. Bernard Lucien[1] entered the seminary at Écône in 1972 and was ordained by Archbishop Lefebvre in 1978. He first published works to demonstrate the contradiction between the teaching of Gregory XVI and Pius IX on freedom of conscience and worship and the teaching of Vatican II on religious liberty. He fundamentally changed his view (a change for which he credits the grace of God) on Christmas 1991 and published a retraction in 1992 to show how this contradiction was merely apparent and not substantial. This led him to regularize his canonical status in 1992; he was incardinated in the archdiocese of Vaduz (Liechtenstein) in 2004 by Archbishop Haas. Since his regularization he has been teaching Thomistic theology in seminaries and houses of formation and has published various works of theology, including for the non-specialist public such as *The Sacred Theology for Beginners and the Initiated* series.

Fr. Antoine-Marie de Araujo was born in 1979 of a Swiss mother and Argentinian father in Geneva, Switzerland, and was raised Catholic. He earned a Master's Degree in Classics at the University of Fribourg (Switzerland), and collaborated on a scholarly edition of Jean Bodin's *Six*

---

[1] See *Spiritu ferventes: Mélanges offerts en l'honneur de l'Abbé Berbard Lucien à l'occasion de son 70e anniversaire* (Poitiers: Dominique Martin Morin, 2022), 573–583.

Books of the Republic (1576). A friend introduced him to the thought of St. Thomas Aquinas, which helped him deepen his faith and commit himself to serving the Church. In 2010 he entered the Fraternity of Saint Vincent Ferrer (FSVF), a traditional religious community inspired by the Dominican spirit, whose priory is located in Chémeré-le-Roi (France), where he was ordained priest in 2019. Fr. Antoine-Marie is secretary of the Fraternity's quarterly review *Sedes Sapientiæ*, and has authored several articles. He is also the editor of two English-language issues of *Sedes Sapientiæ* (2022 and 2024). When not studying theology for his licentiate, Fr. Antoine-Marie preaches to students and goes hiking with scouts.